PASSION
❧ TO ❧
PROSPERITY

INSTANT WAYS TO PROFIT FROM YOUR SKILLS AND TALENTS

MARIA SIMONE

Go to www.IntentionalIncome.com and pick up your

FREE GIFTS Today....

Receive a complete list of my recommended online and offline technology tools and resources, key business contacts, discounted and free services!

www.MariaSimone.com

Free Subscription to "Fast Forward To Success", is a bi-monthly business acceleration ezine offering NEXT STEPS on transforming ideas & talents into revenue and manifest customers with ease.

Step-by-step support to create a 6 or 7 figure business for yourself doing what you love at

www.Passion2Prosperity.com

ACKNOWLEDGMENTS

I would like to acknowledge my loving husband, Michael Murdock, for his ongoing support in helping me share this information with you.

I appreciate Jean Sibley's support in editing my words to make sure my thoughts were accurately conveyed on these pages.

And I am eternally grateful to all my mentors and teachers who pushed and prodded and generally helped inspire my confidence to always "go for it".

TABLE OF CONTENTS

Liability Limits and Disclaimer of Warranty

The author and publisher of this book have used their best efforts in preparing this program and make no warranties with respect to the accuracy, applicability, fitness or completeness of the contents of this program. They disclaim any warranties (expressed or implied), merchantability, or fitness for any particular purpose. The author and publisher shall in no event be held liable for any loss or other damages.

I. CHAPTER ONE ~ABOUT THE AUTHOR

Maria Simone is an entrepreneur, speaker, author, conscious business "architect" and marketing expert who has been featured on ABC News and Fox TV. She has been interviewed for a number of national publications, including Business Week and Inventors Digest. Maria has launched several companies and raised millions of dollars in funding. As a service provider she consistently creates 6-figure incomes, and now helps start-ups and service providers attract experts, customers, resources and capital.

Maria had a successful career in the healthcare industry, starting out as Pharmacist working in one of the largest trauma hospitals in New York City in 1986 before moving into healthcare administration and sales. She consulted for some of the top pharmaceutical firms in the country and negotiated multi-million dollar contracts. By 1998, she had contemplated making some radical changes and committed at that time to striking out on her own. She learned how to continually surround herself with the right people, how to fund any project she worked on, and how to skillfully leverage and capitalize on her ideas and talents. In 1998, Maria retired from the healthcare industry and stepped into the new income streams she had quickly created for herself.

Since 1992, Maria has started several businesses, licensed her ideas for royalties, and raised over $1 million dollars for herself and others. Her products have been featured on department store shelves, including Macy's and Bloomingdales. She has sold companies she created, as well as sold companies with which she has an ongoing, active relationship.

Maria and her husband Michael live in beautiful Scottsdale, Arizona.

⌘ ⌘ ⌘

"...in the blink of an eye you might reinvent yourself... the person you were yesterday might not be the person you are tomorrow."

~~Jodi Picoult

II. CHAPTER TWO ~ INTRODUCTION

Welcome! My name is Maria Simone and I am excited that you're reading this valuable book I've prepared for you. I'm *thrilled* that you have decided to take the next step in growing your business and sharing your talents with the world!

Before we begin, let me share with you how I evolved from a corporate career into my multifaceted and lucrative entrepreneurial world of today. I started out as a pharmacist in New York in 1986 after graduating with a B.S. in Pharmacy from St. John's University. In my hospital career, I worked in the intensive care and coronary care units of one of the largest trauma hospitals in New York City. In 1990, I transitioned into management positions in home health care. My responsibilities included negotiating large provider contracts with insurance companies. I discovered that I *loved* the art of deal making! During that period, I also consulted for some top pharmaceutical firms in the country and co-authored Pharmacy Statutes for the state of Arizona.

My talent was to look at any situation and create value for all involved, as well as put together joint ventures. I could go into physician's offices or clinics, look at how they were providing services, and see the value they were bringing to patients and customers. I helped them create additional profit centers to add even more value for their patients and increase their revenues.

I was so successful at this, I decided to go out on my own and put "deals" together for myself. In 1999, I retired my professional license and transitioned from health care to business consulting. Since that time, I've started four businesses, raised millions in funding, licensed inventions (my ideas), and I have seen my products sold at Macy's and other stores. I've helped thousands of people access the resources they need to create the business of their dreams, and done this very consciously, all the while taking their passions and goals into consideration. It has been very exciting for me, and now I want to help *you!*

Was it always easy for me? No! I had many ups and downs. My business life finally transformed because I took the time to get the answers I needed, and develop the skills necessary to succeed. I'd like to convey some of what I learned to you. My goal in this E-Book is to not only tell you how you can organize your talents into new products and services, but to also show you how to market those products and services to serve more people.

I believe that **prosperity is directly proportional to how well you serve others, and how good you feel about yourself**. Give yourself permission to have it all! If you're passionate about what you're doing, taking it to another level is a fun and exciting journey!

I have to admit, I am presenting a lot of information to you in this book. What you're about to read results from years and years of study, being mentored, discovering what works by just doing, and trial and error. I recommend you go through the materials, especially those you'll find by registering your book at www.intentionalincome.com. Become inspired to get your own creative juices flowing, and start giving yourself permission to have it all!

At the end of this book, I help you create a Strategic Action Plan. Your plan will indicate the next steps to take and prevent overwhelm. I recommend taking in the information, processing it, feeling what resonates with you, going through a few action steps and then simply *start creating*. Start creating products for yourself, start working with some of the marketing tools I'm about to give you... and just start '*doing*'. You'll plan some of this out, but I highly encourage you to get out there and begin having the experiences that will help guide you to your next step.

Many years ago, as I began my entrepreneurial journey, I realized I could learn everything there is to know about business, but if I didn't also become more self-aware, and understand the role spirituality and universal wisdom played in my life and *especially* if I *mistrusted* the success I was experiencing, my success would be short-lived.

I learned to ALLOW success to happen and *not to sabotage* the ever-growing abundance I was creating for myself. I encourage you to get to know yourself as well, and become aware of how you're feeling as we unfold your new success plan in the following pages.

⌘ ⌘ ⌘

Simple awareness causes a shift...taking action creates a transformation!

~~Maria Simone

III. CHAPTER THREE ~ STRATEGIES FOR GETTING STARTED

A. Vision

First, it's very important to get in touch with your vision. This is all about YOU. We need to wrap a business around you, your passion, and your joy. Never forget this!

Consider this opportunity a wonderful fork in the road of your life. You've just been given a *free pass* to create the life of your dreams from this point onward, regardless of your prior experience. You don't have to know all the "how to" right now. Simply *commit* to letting it happen!

What do you want your life to look like? What are your personal expectations and desires? For a long time you may have been living by default---working in jobs just to make money, or you may have liked what you were doing but lost your passion and didn't know what to do next.

Do you have *outside influencers* consciously or subconsciously dictating how to run your life? Have you Held *preconceived notions* about how to earn an income? How hard you're supposed to work for it?

There have been times I've worked with a client to show them an easier path to create revenue, yet they seem very attached to a belief that hard work is needed to achieve their goals. They sometimes find it difficult to release this belief and embrace a less complicated, easier way to create new income. This could be as simple as allowing others to support you with their time and resources, or creating revenue that's recurring rather then a one-time event.

As you are reading this, perhaps you are just getting started. Maybe you're transitioning from one career and trying to see what's next for you. You're out there looking for new opportunities, figuring out what makes you tick, and exploring what you're passionate about. That is great. I hope to inspire you in this book to *take action*!

You have to start somewhere. Many years ago, when I decided to leave my corporate career and start my own business, I wasn't sure what I wanted to do. I just knew that *something had to change*. The first and only action I could take was to COMMIT to allowing myself to find something new that I would love to do.

I didn't know *what* it was going to be or *how* it was going to happen. Once I committed to making this change, I was able to allow myself to have new experiences, meet new people, and acquire new skills in a short period of time. I quickly stepped into new profitable activities that I *enjoyed* doing instead of just finding a way to make money.

You may be currently in business and offering certain services or talents to people, but would like to diversify. This is a good time to take stock. Which aspects of your work do you love? What types of people do you like to be around? Truly get in touch with yourself and what you want to create in your life, regardless of how far fetched it may seem at this moment. Remember, the "how-to" will always show up right after you decide on the "what".

B. Why make changes

Understand why you are asking yourself these key questions about vision and change. Decide where you fit in so you can develop a strategy based on your professional goals:

1. Are you a *service professional* who wants to create additional and residual income through information products? Packaging your talents allows you to create more of a business instead of you 'owning' a job. It allows you to create revenue far beyond what you can do by trading time for dollars. Have you realized that the best visioning and planning isn't really about making money? The whole focus of my work with you is for you to be positioned to *serve more people*.

Doesn't it make sense that if you're passionate about doing something, and that's your primary goal, you do more of it? This is a natural way for you to do more of what you love, serve more people, and make a difference in their lives. The money is secondary, and will flow if you are in tune with your passion, how to package your talents, and how to serve more people.

I began consulting with individual companies on my own time while I was working full time for a large home health firm. It was great way to create additional income, but it still took time. When I ventured out on my own, I knew that consulting as a primary revenue stream wouldn't serve me for very long, so I quickly began creating multiple revenue streams packaging my talents and my ideas. The residual income came from putting lucrative contracts together, fees from an idea I licensed out to a natural products company, and overrides from various affiliate relationships.

2. Are you an existing *business owner*? Perhaps you sell one product classification and want to diversify. Diversifying your products and services lets you build value in your company, which, in turn, attracts lucrative strategic alliances and contracts.

What's the point of your business? Are you in a business assuming it will continue for the rest of your life? Is there a legacy you'd like to build up and turn over to your family? What's your *exit strategy*? Do you want to sell your company some day? Are you thinking of possibly franchising or expanding nationally in other ways?

People who create successful businesses create with the *end in mind*. If you haven't considered your exit strategies, now is a perfect time. In any case, thinking bigger doesn't necessarily mean you'll have to work harder. With my type of success plan in place, you'll simply work *smarter*, not harder, as you grow.

C. Understand your target market

Who is your target market and what do they want? It's critical for you to identify and describe your ideal customer. The more niched and specific you are, the easier it becomes to market your services and products. There are many people I speak to who are struggling to put products together, or to market their products and services. They come to me for advice and say, "What do you think about me creating this product?"

> I say, "Who is your target market?"
> They reply, "Well, I don't know."
> I say, *"Time to find out!"*

Before you can create a product, it's very important to understand to whom you're marketing and wanting to sell your products or services. If you don't know, I highly recommend you spend time finding your answer.

You can narrow your niche down to a group that is the "hungriest" for what you offer. Who has an immediate sense of urgency for your solution? Pro-boxers for a healing device? People in pre-foreclosure for debt relief? Is it a certain demographic, such as men or women in a certain age bracket or a certain industry, or those with a specific problem you can address?

Spend time at this stage personally talking to your potential target market. Ask what your potential and current customers want. Then start narrowing in on that niche. I want you to develop your niche first and then branch out. Don't worry that you'll exclude anyone by doing this. It's not true that if you create products specific to one market, it excludes other people or has a detrimental effect on your business. The opposite is true! *The more niched you are, the easier it becomes to tap into that market.* Later on you can create similar products and services for another niche market.

You'll actually become the expert to a certain market segment and start seeing many referrals. Just consider --- if you were experiencing chest pains, wouldn't you rather see a cardiologist as opposed to a primary care physician? Psychologically, you want to immediately go to the expert in that field. That's what I want you to become – an expert in your particular niche market. People will develop an immediate connection with you.

D. Brand YOU

I recommend starting the process of branding YOU, if you haven't done so already. You want to work on having YOU stand out, getting YOU noticed. You become the celebrity in your field. What's your *story*? What's *unique* to you?

People connect with people, so make sure that there is a *personal* connection and your *fingerprint is all over your business.* This is especially important when you're starting out. Create a vision statement for yourself and your company to provide focus, and for your branding to revolve around. Ultimately, your goal is to communicate **big and bold** with descriptive **benefits** that stand out and are seen by many people.

Learn to *dominate* your market. What powerful, truthful, claims can you make about the benefits you have to offer someone? If I say I'm a business consultant, it's not as powerful as announcing that I'm the "Passion To Prosperity Diva"!

Imagine you were hungry for a burger and came across two restaurants, one with a sign saying "Hamburgers" and the other with a sign saying "The BEST Hamburgers in town" or "VOTED BEST Hamburgers". Chances are you'd choose "The BEST Hamburgers" or "VOTED BEST Hamburgers". Boldness has its appeal and if you weren't even hungry for a burger at the time, you might change your mind after seeing the sign!

E. Costs of customer acquisition

We all have customer acquisition costs in our businesses. You may not be paying attention to that number right now, but it exists and you need to work with it.

Get in touch with what the costs are to acquire a new customer, as well as how much each customer invests with you *over the life* of that relationship. This helps determine which specific products you'll be able to give away, as well as the marketing tactics you employ.

This is a good time to sit down and go over all your activities – all the time and expense it takes to market yourself. What is invested in you actually acquiring new customers? In this process you'll find that whatever that acquisition cost is, we will actually lower it to position you for greater profitability without having to produce a significant increase in revenue. Also, by understanding your acquisition costs, and subsequently how much a customer is worth to you, you'll know which programs work best for you to market.

I have learned to be very generous and giving in my marketing efforts to attract prospective customers, because I've discovered that people who experience me on some level often like to continue working with me for a long period of time. One of my clients had a million dollar business, yet found they weren't seeing those dollars going into their bank account and were therefore still struggling to make ends meet. There were several reasons for this, but the main one was that the costs to acquire each of their customers were almost EQUAL to the value of each customer in the purchases they made. After my consultations, they started immediately refining their sales and marketing process, which included appearances at tradeshows and implementing an online program. You may find yourself that you make considerable efforts, but the long term gain isn't there. Knowing this will help you refine and target your marketing activities.

Customer acquisition costs are important numbers to work with as you develop new products and services. The higher a customer's value to you, the more you should invest in acquiring and retaining that customer. There are several ways to arrive at this number. The table below shows one way of arriving at your customer acquisition costs.

⌘ ⌘ ⌘

Customer Acquisition Costs		
	Per month	Per year
Advertising		
Tradeshows		
Travel		
PR activities		
Miscellaneous sales and marketing expenses		
TOTAL EXPENSES		
# OF CUSTOMERS		
BASIC acquisition cost = TOTAL EXPENSES divided by # OF CUSTOMERS		
REVENUE		
Average Value of customer = REVENUE divided by # OF CUSTOMERS		

"Strange is our situation here upon earth. Each of us comes for a short visit, not knowing why, yet sometimes seeming to a divine purpose...Many times a day I realize how much my outer and inner life is built upon the labors of people, both living and dead, and how earnestly I must exert myself in order to give in return as much as I have received."

~~Albert Einstein

IV. CHAPTER FOUR ~ CREATE A POWER TEAM TO OPEN DOORS AND MAKE THINGS HAPPEN

As the saying goes, and I'm sure you've said this yourself many times, "If I only knew *then* what I know *now*, my life would be *so much easier*."

I say **"Why wait to have the experience"**??!!!

If we want to avoid unpleasant experiences or less than desirable outcomes, it makes sense to know as much as possible about each experience we are about to have. Make sure we have all the facts, know our options, best and worse case scenarios, and manage expectations. Isn't that why we read Consumer Reports before making a car or electronics purchase, buy baby books when we're expecting, or talk to people in real estate before purchasing a home?

These concepts don't always translate to the entrepreneur starting a business. Sure, launching a business is an exciting adventure, but if you haven't been down that path before, it can be a perilous journey to take alone. Avoid the "hard knocks" that people insist on having by building a TEAM of people that have demonstrated success in the relevant areas for your business. I'm not talking about Aunt Sally who just adores you and wants to help. Save those lovely people for Thanksgiving dinners. I mean people who have really accomplished something in your industry and now *you are going down the same path they have.*

One of the biggest mistakes I see people make in launching their business is that they are all excited about moving forward yet operate in a VOID. Working without a net. Entering uncharted waters without a compass. You get the drift.

When I'm about to work with someone, I first get details about the financial and other goals they may have regarding their business. The next few questions and their responses are often like this:

ME: Have you ever achieved these revenue goals before?
THEM: No.

ME: Have you ever had products in the marketplace like this before?
THEM: No.

ME: Do you know exactly what you're doing?
THEM: Not really. but I'm really excited and I'm sure I'll find out what I need to know.

What if you knew in advance how to get from point A to point B in the shortest period of time? With the least amount of resistance by harnessing the expertise and credibility of those who have taken a similar journey?

In the following pages, I elaborate for you how to take the simpler, better informed path. I tell you who to go to, what to say and how to tap into the wealth of information and contacts at your disposal. I guarantee that you'll find yourself saying less and less "If I only knew then what I know now."

Objectives of having a team

Ideally, you want to attract people who resonate with you and can get behind your ideas and your passion. You want to always "aim high" with regard to credentials, experience, and/or reputation. You not only want to attract the most talent you could possibly have, but those are the people that will generally be willing to work for little or no compensation in exchange for helping you realize your dream.

You want to have the opportunity to create a professional relationship with them. They should be available periodically to answer questions you may have, validate some of your ideas and concepts, give direction as to what path to take, introduce you to other resources, and become a "magnet" for you in that their association with your project attracts attention from your industry or customer base. This is similar to the attraction power of having a celebrity attached to a charitable event.

We will call this group your "Advisory Team" --- not to be confused with a Board of Directors, which is a more formal business arrangement. Some people call their Team "Mastermind Group" or "Mentor Group". I have used all of these terms in my life, but if it relates to business, I prefer Advisory Team.

Your Advisory Team should be supportive and inspiring and allow you to feel confident in your abilities as you move forward. You want your Team to provide contrast as much as possible so that you are viewing a situation from many angles. People who always 'say yes' are not helpful, yet if there is too much resistance in the relationship, replace them as soon as possible. You are on a long journey and you have the right to have as much fun as you can stand and to surround yourself with only the nicest people. They should not be competitive with you, but support you and help pave the way for an easier ride.

Prepare yourself to manifest

It's important to understand that the people you attract will be a total reflection of how YOU are "showing up". If you are needy, lack confidence, lack passion, want to be taken care of, or haven't put yourself in a position to receive support -- you will attract those who don't have your best interest at heart, or you may actually repel the very people you need.

It is important to prepare yourself to receive support but not be needy for it. You are not expected to "know everything" - that is what your Team is for, but you should exhibit confidence and articulate your passion at every turn.

That is the fuel that will drive these relationships --- not your business --- and the more responsibility you take for that, the faster you will succeed.

There are many times I am working with someone and it is apparent that they have an incredible invention or a great opportunity before them. However, if they lack confidence or it appears they "get in their way" by sabotaging their efforts, my recommendation is to do some personal development work. The deepest, fastest and most intense personal transformational programs I have ever encountered (and continue to benefit from) are weekend workshops facilitated by Esperanza Universal at the SOUL Institute. You can register for a free teleclass to start experiencing the benefits they have to offer at www.masteringyourlife.com . Let them know I referred you!

You are the driving force behind your business, not your product, so you want to be in a position where you can easily manifest success on many levels and attract, not repel, the very people and things that can help you tremendously on your journey.

Let's move on to our strategies for building an amazing Advisory Team!

STRATEGY #1: Define and visualize who should be on your team

Ideally, you would want to have at least 3-4 people that have demonstrated success in the areas that you are most concentrated on RIGHT NOW. Examples of the credentials that would be most desirable:

1. Someone with experience in developing a business --- starting a business, acquiring funding, managing legalities of a business, growth and exit strategies, and so on. They can help you with advice on legal structure, business planning issues, investor relations (if any), and operations. Be most concerned about their business development expertise, not necessarily industry credentials (although having both is a plus). For example, I have people on my Team that do not have experience in my industry but they have built companies with revenues that were in excess of $20 million.

2. Someone that has actually launched or worked with a company that has achieved your desired revenue goals in yours or a similar industry. Ideally, you want someone that built and sold a successful business within your industry, retired from their position, held a key management role or a Board of Director's post. Perhaps they were a high level sales or finance director.

For example, one of my companies is a fashion accessory company so I sought out the advice of Nick Graham who had founded the very successful *Joe Boxer* brand during the 80's. *Joe Boxer* was one of the companies I was modeling mine after so it made sense that I would want to speak with him.

3. Someone that responsibly represents YOUR desired market that can give you feedback and credibility along the way. This could be someone on the inside track with your customers, someone well respected, an icon or celebrity perhaps. For example, my friends invented an automotive device and were able to get the endorsement and advisement of the editor of Motor Trend Magazine during their launch phase. I was very fortunate to have the former CEO of Macy's on my Team as I was launching my fashion company. Since my customers were the Macy's buyers, it really helped us get a foot in the door, not to mention the priceless feedback we received on product development.

4. You may consider having someone on your Team that has nothing to do with business but whom acts as a buffer for you, lets you vent and helps you have balance in your life. Someone who offers you a different perspective. I recommend not choosing a family member, as they have a tendency to get too protective, however you don't want

someone that is heavily connected to your business.

5. As you progress, you will develop Teams of people that will work "in" your business (for example, Sales, Operations). For the purposes of organizing a new business, your Team will be working "on" your business.

You will want to take these profiles and apply them to your own unique business and industry. You may decide to have more people on your Team, but word to the wise, it does get crowded! You may personally have some of the experiences listed above and therefore prefer to create a different profile. The important thing to remember is that you need a diverse group of individuals with well-rounded talents and with experience beyond yours (REMEMBER: "if I only knew then...") to support you at whatever stage you are at in the success continuum.

STRATEGY #2: Compelling the right people to say "Yes"

Now that you've identified who you would like to have on your Team, it's important to put yourself in a position to attract these people.

It usually happens that when I am working with someone and we have identified their ideal Team members, these people start crossing their path. Law of Attraction is at work for you here. It's true. They meet them serendipitously at an event, they are introduced to them by a third party, they attend an event where the person in question is a speaker, or the opportunity arises to just contact them directly.

You have a profile of what type of credentials and expertise they may have but may not have a "face" yet. Focus on the profile – keep putting it out there that you would like to meet this type of person and the "face" will show up for you. Most of the time, once the profile is identified, people realize that the actual *person* is already in their life.

Years ago when I was modeling one of my companies after the *Joe Boxer* brand, I didn't actually know who any of the principals were until one day my then-partner attended an event where Nick Graham, the founder of *Joe Boxer*, was speaking and we made the connection. The following week, we attended a charity event and ran into him yet again. At that time I had the opportunity to connect with him and ask for some time to meet. It can really be that easy.

Other ways to find the "face" is to read your local paper and see "who's doing what" in business. Aim high, remember? The people you want on your team are the ones who get written up in the paper when they retire, switch companies, organize a charity event, speak at an event, and so on.   The internet is a great source of course for this type of info. Search away!

Also make plans to network with different groups of people so that you may be introduced to them. There are many high level CEO type groups out there that I would recommend getting connected to at some level. They provide instant access to many movers and shakers in your industry. Check in with people in your industry to identify these people. Do you have an automotive product? Fashion? Health and Beauty? Business service? Go to those people and find out who they know in that industry or who is most admired. Go to trade shows in your industry and meet some of these people directly. A great resource for finding any tradeshow in any industry is at http://www.tsnn.com . Use the search bar up top to find a show then go "walk the show". Exhibition areas are usually free and provide a source of valuable contacts. I even find great resumes at http://www.craigslist.org of all places.

"Maria, why would these people want to help ME?"

Why not?

People who have reached certain levels of success and accomplishment have a strong feeling of gratitude and generally feel very blessed. Those are the people you want to meet. The "cup is overflowing" and there is a general sense of urgency about giving something back. That's why I've given this information to you for free today, why I mentor others, and why I participate in so many charitable activities. Believe me, THEY are looking for YOU.

So what do you do next?

Once you have made the connection, you will want to schedule a short meeting with this person. Preferably in person for 30 minutes or LESS. If they offer more time or can have a meal with you, go for it. These are usually very busy people with many demands for their time and expertise. You clearly stating that you will not be requiring more than 30 minutes of their time sends a very positive message that you are safe to meet.

Prepare at least 3-5 questions that they are uniquely qualified to address. Don't bog them down with too many details about your business or other aspects of your business that don't pertain to them. Some suggestions on what to ask:

1. Their validation or nod of approval for what you're working on. Do they see this taking off?
2. What could you do to speed up the process?
3. What would they do next if they were in your shoes?
4. Is there anything to be most concerned about at this stage?
5. Is there anything they would change in your plan?
6. Are there other people they know that could help?
7. Any other advice they could give?

If you feel that this person is hesitant about supporting you, is too harsh perhaps, too competitive or you are generally not enjoying the personal interaction (if what they are saying is difficult for you to hear, that's another story), I would end the meeting at the appointed time and thank them for their effort. At least send a thank you note afterwards.

If they have been forthcoming with the information you asked for and you felt a connection with this person, I recommend taking it to the next level.

1. End the meeting at the time you promised unless your guest gives you permission to or would clearly like to continue the conversation. Make it obvious by mentioning it and getting verbal feedback. Don't make assumptions at your first meeting.

2. Next, ask for their permission to check in with them via email or phone once a month so that you could share your progress with them. Sincerely let them know how much it would mean to you ---- which it should --- to consider them as a virtual advisor.

3. Be very clear that this is not an official position in your company and should take no longer than 15 minutes a month at this stage. You can mention that there is no formal paperwork required of them nor any other obligations besides the monthly check in. You may feel more comfortable preparing

a very simple Letter of Intent. I mention it later on.

4. Compensation is not offered here and will probably not be brought up in conversation. Do not mention it in this conversation. It is important to state that you would consider it an honor to have someone with their credentials in your corner that you could ask a question of periodically. Make plans to have a program in place at some point, either with stock, cash or some other award, that your Team members will benefit from when your business is more stable.

Once you have clearly stated what the expectations are of them, the time involved and expressed your gratitude, people will most often say YES to this request.

If possible during this encounter, it would be very beneficial to you if they could provide a bio of sorts for you to have on file. Most people can verbally give you a few lines to use, email you their written version or in many cases, you can pull something off their website or from the internet. You will want to use this information in your planning or marketing process later on.

Take a moment at this point to celebrate your accomplishment! You are now receiving the priceless support of someone who has taken the journey you are about to take. Your chances for success have just increased tremendously!

STRATEGY #3: Maintain momentum

Once you have your team in place it is important to maintain ongoing communication with them, to keep them abreast of your progress, to capitalize on their suggestions and contacts, and to inform others of your relationship. I'll show you how to do that in a moment.

A quick note about maintaining a high degree of integrity in your business and protecting your intellectual assets:

As you start interacting more and more with members of your Team (and anyone else involved in your business), you will likely share confidential information and want to have other agreements in place. One of the best software purchases I've ever made was Agreement Builder by Jian . This tool contains over 130 templates for all kinds of contracts, business letters, and legal forms such as Non-Disclosure Agreements, Work-For-Hire, and a variety of Applications. We use the tools daily in our office. I recommend making the purchase and start accessing the templates TODAY because you want to immediately be able to communicate a high degree of professionalism to anyone you interact with in your business, not to mention having the tools to ensure protection of your intellectual assets.

Follow-up with your team:

1. Schedule your monthly "meetings" to keep them abreast of any new developments and

to seek their ongoing advice and support. As the relationship progresses, you'll find they will be willing to give you more and more time.

2. Prepare a short, positive, upbeat monthly communication that goes out to your Team via email that specifically addresses your progress, new developments and most especially WHAT YOU NEED NEXT to help you move forward. This is not a consumer sales piece or newsletter. This is specifically related to the development of your business infrastructure.

3. Consider getting the group together, virtually or live at some point to have a monthly brainstorming session. If you do not have conferencing capabilities in place, sign up for a conference line at http://www.nocostconfrence.com.com . Order the recording features – it's all free.

4. Implement their ideas as much as possible if you feel they are appropriate for you.

5. Request additional contacts and support from your team as they get to know you and are clear about the direction you are taking.

6. Be prepared to be connected to investors, sales channels, customers, marketing, media opportunities and many other resources as time goes by. You can expect it!

7. Express gratitude often, and remember that their commitment to you is directly proportional to YOUR passion and commitment to YOURSELF and your project.

Summary

People often think they need money to launch a business or create something new. I have learned it's not the money at all --- it's the people you really need. I envision my Team to be "magnets" that, when held up and positioned properly, will attract the investors that I need, the customers I desire, and strategic alliances with resource providers that will help take me to the next level. Consider this:

- I would be more inclined to invest in an internet start-up company if someone on the Team had been part of the founding group of Google, Microsoft, Apple or EBay.

- I would be more inclined to buy a product from a company I may not know if someone else whom I respected was endorsing it.

- I would be more interested in doing a strategic alliance arrangement with an unknown company if someone on the Team was known for putting together very lucrative, win-win, strategic partnerships.

You will probably be faced with all of these scenarios someday and very often the deciding factor, as you can see, is "who's on your TEAM!" So take the time now to start cultivating these relationships right from the beginning and you will MANIFEST SUCCESS sooner than you had imagined!

⌘ ⌘ ⌘

"Successful people turn everyone who can help them into mentors!"

~~John Crosby

V. CHAPTER FIVE ~ GET PEOPLE TO TAKE ACTION

The creation of your sales and marketing funnel ("customer pipeline") is a standard technique in the sales world. I update it for you in this book, to make it applicable to your situation, as well as include current, proven online tools and technologies. I have personally honed and integrated an effective funnel into my businesses, and it has made all the difference in the world. As you implement a funnel like mine, you'll also create an automated system with the potential to reach masses of new prospects! This type of funnel is created for optimal success in today's exciting web-oriented world.

As you start putting your programs together, always keep your own sales funnel in mind. No matter what revenue stream you decide to incorporate into your life, you should always have a steady stream of potential customers to interact with, and that's exactly what the sales funnel model provides for you.

What does a sales funnel look like and how does it work? A sales funnel looks like a funnel in the physical world. As the sample funnel in this book shows, the wide opening is at the top of the page, and the narrow end is at the bottom. At the top are services and products that involve only a small amount of time or money from you and your prospect, such as a Special Report. As prospects start interacting with you and believing in you, they progressively invest more to benefit from your services and products and they go down the funnel to your premium offerings.

You can start small, using basic components, but it's best to create something that can ultimately be scaled up. Interested prospects will take action to find out more about you. At that time, give them a compelling reason to stick around ---let them take advantage of an irresistible offer or a gift. For example, as a service professional, you instruct people to call for a free consultation before they purchase services from you. This action can be very limiting to your practice, however. Ultimately it's in your best interest to lead them to your website for a written, audio or video overview that explains your service and who you are, thereby reducing the 1-on-1 time you would otherwise have spent.

Here are the key activities in creating a successful marketing funnel:

A. Perform sales, marketing, and PR activities to attract potential customers

Where is the point of contact with a prospect? Typically this happens when they sign in at your website or blog, email you requesting information, return a postcard that was mailed to them requesting more information, phone you, or give you a business card. This first point of contact is at the widest opening of your funnel.

B. Create a compelling offer

Your prospects should leave their contact info for continued communication and they'll usually do that if you offer something worthwhile in return, such as a free newsletter subscription, a coupon, a resource list, or a free book. Your offer needs to be prominently placed and clearly displayed for your prospects to take action.

I offer something compelling at each of my websites in exchange for personal contact information. You can experience this at www.cityscarves.com and www.passion2prosperity.com. When people arrive at my City Scarves site, they may not be ready to purchase a silk scarf but they often download a free scarf-tying lesson, which is very relevant to why they came to my site in the first place. People buy from people they know and trust. Develop a relationship with your prospects and customers. Provide information, education and value on an ongoing basis through regular communication with your subscribers. Do this with regular email follow-up, direct mail, or telephone. I describe these techniques in the following pages.

C. Introduce them to your products and services

Offer prospects the opportunity to buy products and services to improve some aspect of their life. If possible, begin offering lower price point items so they experience you without risk and without much thought to their investment. As they become more invested in the relationship, they more readily invest at higher price points.

D. Complete a sale and then offer more products and services

Create opportunities for people to continue to experience you with additional product and service offerings. Ideally, these are complimentary and may include continuity or recurring revenue.

E. Create a referral program for existing customers

Your existing customers can be your *greatest sales force* and that's why it is important to take care of them. Offer special rewards, perks and discounts to help motivate your customers to refer to you.

The goal of this process is to draw as many people into your funnel as possible through prospecting and marketing to build a solid subscriber base of potential customers with whom you can interact. The selling process happens more naturally as you establish your credibility and develop relationships with prospects.

Building a subscriber list is a *critical, primary function* for you, no matter what business you're in!

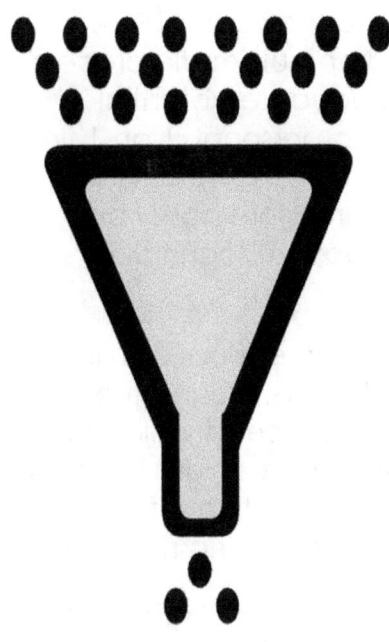

F. Sample Sales and Marketing Funnel

<<<Prospective customers are introduced to your brand through marketing, advertising and PR efforts.

<<< They arrive at your website or interact with you long enough to turn over their contact info because they want to learn more and/or have received something of value. Freebies are featured here.

<<<Become active customers when they begin to buy your products and services after receiving communications about the benefits of working with you/ buying your product. Lower price points here.

<<< A few will progress to your "premium" products or services.

Many people don't know how powerful a sales and marketing funnel like mine can be. Those who don't know how to successfully implement this type of funnel in their business are probably working TOO hard because they don't have a strategic action plan and an automatic process set up to pre-qualify and educate potential customers. They're investing personal, 1-on-1 time networking and prospecting for customers and performing activities that are more costly and time consuming than the passive techniques employed with a funnel.

If you're the one providing the education, giving materials to potential customers, closing the sale and possibly providing the service as well, you'll appreciate this concept! You'll see your business take off once you start implementing a funnel like mine, which incorporates automating many of these steps.

The beautiful part is you get to clone yourself! Let's evaluate aspects of what you do and what you love to do. I want you to package what you offer in different ways to help people experience you on many levels *before* they interact with you personally. You get to reach out to *many more* people because it's not you personally providing this service. This is the *beauty* of it. Instead, you'll use the marketing techniques and programs and create your own marketing funnel.

Have you noticed I minimize the concept of "selling" in the traditional sense? Yes, something is being bought and something sold. But if you do your marketing and sales very consciously --- in a way that makes people feel supported, understood, more educated, and more aware of your value, your customers will ultimately make their own decisions to buy your products and services. It's a process you are going to put on autopilot. *How cool is that!*

As we're going through this process, pinpoint the products and services you want to include in your sales funnel, as well as the marketing programs you want to initiate.

⌘ ⌘ ⌘

"You are the embodiment of the information you choose to accept and act upon. To change your circumstances, you need to change your thinking and subsequent actions"

~~Adlin Sinclair

VI. CHAPTER SIX ~ JAY ABRAHAM'S "POWER PARTHENON PRINCIPLE"

I had the very good fortune several years ago of being personally mentored by Jay Abraham, one of the country's foremost marketing experts, and I highly recommend learning more about his marketing wisdom. A key principle I learned from Jay is the Power Parthenon Principle. Incorporating this principle and others into my business model *dramatically* changed my results, and I know they can do the same for you.

There are three basic ways to build revenues in any type of business, whether it is retail, service oriented, wholesale or an information products business. As you build on each of the following principles, you'll experience exponential growth in your business.

A. Develop new customers

This is the primary way that most people build their businesses--- and it is also the *costliest*. It involves all the elements of the sales and marketing funnel --- prospecting, advertising, PR, and so on. Many businesses focus on this aspect day in and day out as the primary, and sometimes the *only*, means of developing sales. While this is necessary for new businesses, I recommend you also focus on the other principles as you mature and work with an existing customer base.

B. Offer more products and services to existing customers

Very often a company has one or two products they offer customers and they're in a *continual* process of developing new customers. It's much more cost-effective to explore the needs of your existing customer base and develop additional products and services to offer them. (That's actually very exciting for me! I *love* to create those programs for myself and others!)

Instead of creating *more* products, focus on how to OFFER additional products and services. This is where affiliate and joint venture alliances fit in nicely. I want to explain how you do that, as it's a great way to quickly build more revenue in your business without having to develop new customers.

C. Encourage existing customers to refer people they know

This is one of the most cost-effective ways of developing your business. Offer wonderful incentives, motivations, and rewards to existing and loyal customers and make them feel totally supported and appreciated by you. They'll be inspired to refer others to you if they have enjoyed their experience with you.

I know many businesses that are very successful because they implemented outstanding referral programs. Referrals make up the foundation of their business. They invest in *hardly any advertising or additional marketing outside of their existing customer base.* Many techniques discussed in this book allow you to create your own active referral program and you'll be wonderfully surprised how much success is possible with referrals!

As you can see, there are at least three legs of business development to focus on as a means of increasing your revenue. Obviously you can't do it all at once, but little by little, as you get each of these up and running, you'll experience continual and exponential growth. I can assure you this will happen and it will be very exciting for you!

⌘　⌘　⌘

"Take up one idea, make that one idea your life – think or it, dream of it, and live on that idea. Let the brain, muscles, nerves, every part of your body, be full of that idea, and just leave every other idea alone. This is the way to success. That is the way spiritual giants are produced."

~~Swami Vivekananda

VII. CHAPTER SEVEN ~ DEVELOPING REVENUE STREAMS

A. Get clear on your purpose

In this section we discuss some sample products and services to wrap around your core talents, skills and experiences. At this point, you should have an idea *why* you're creating multiple products and services. Many service providers *trade time for dollars*, which *greatly* limits their revenue potential.

By creating more products and services, you increase your revenue because you're literally *cloning* yourself. People will be able to experience more of you without you having to work one-on-one. Once these items are created, they can be sold over and over again. You won't have to constantly reinvent the wheel anymore!

Another reason to create some free or lower cost products and services is to *fill your funnel*. Give people the opportunity to start experiencing you before they actually engage your services or invest at a higher price point. Case in point: many service providers go through a fairly lengthy educational process of describing the features and benefits of what they're doing and then developing a relationship with a potential client.

If you have created other products and services that express you, and can be used to educate the consumer, the time you are spending with a prospect can be shortened. Realize that you may not need direct contact with a potential customer prior to the actual engagement. It's going to *save you a lot of time!* Believe me, great results will come from filling your funnel and developing new revenue streams based on what you know and love to do!

Are you a connector or networker without your own products to offer and want to quickly build new revenue streams? Consider selling and promoting other people's products as well as making connections for people that provide profit for you. I did this for years prior to developing my own "brand" of products and launching my own inventions.

B. 45 potential products and services to create

These potential products and services include online as well as offline products and services, as this section discusses the retail sector.

1. Ezine or electronic newsletter

An ezine, or electronic magazine sent out regularly, is one of the most important communication tools any business can have today. It's the perfect way to enroll people into your marketing funnel and should be your most basic communication with anyone who crosses your path.

This product takes many forms, depending on what you're trying to convey and whether you offer it as a paid subscription to create revenue or as a free marketing tool. I recommend it as a communication tool. Send it out at least once a month---preferably once a week.

Some people send out very simple plain text email messages with no graphics and there are also templates with all the bells and whistles. Set up a template of your layout or get a virtual assistant to help you. Once the ezine template is set up, which is not difficult, it's very easy to send out repeatedly with new content.

Many people offer an ezine as a complimentary subscription, moving into a more content-rich paid ezine subscription later on. You need an automated vehicle, called an autoresponder, to send it out. The resources I recommend for simple autoresponder services with built-in newsletter templates are at www.intentionalincome.com

What kind of *content* should be in your ezine? Provide mostly *value-added* content with some product or service offerings. I recommend your promotions be less than 40%, with 60% providing educational or other value. Education, strategies, how-to's, secret tips, sharing personal experiences, giving something away, resource links, and alerts could all work well with prospective customers.

Content is determined by your *target market* and *what they want to see*. Provide a tip of the month, or just share something relevant to their industry. Remember, the purpose of your ezine is to communicate regularly with your target market.

The ezine doesn't have to be something you personally write if you don't have the talent or time. What I've done with several ezines I've published is to use the content of other contributors, and I always give my contributors full credit.

It's wise to include some content that promotes what you're doing. Maybe you're having a special sale or you just want to remind them of your products or services. You can also use your ezine as the vehicle to market other resources. I often post links to providers of resources relevant to my target market. Take it a step further by selling advertising to these providers to further monetize your ezine.

If you already sell products or services, use a shopping cart technology with built-in newsletter features. In addition to newsletter/ezine delivery capabilities, a good shopping cart has other integrated features, such as your product catalog, affiliate modules, sales tracking mechanisms, follow-up autoresponders (ongoing message system), and connection to payment gateways.

How does the process work? People come to your website and fill out your online form requesting more information. The information goes right into the shopping cart and a pre-programmed message gets delivered to thank them and give them any information you'd like to provide at this point.

Go to www.intentionalincome.com for my recommended resources for producing your ezine.

2. Group Teleclass

A very popular way to package yourself is to host teleclasses or group telephone conference calls. Teleclass technology has developed for several years and become very low cost and user-friendly. Many formerly 'live' speaking and seminar events have now gone on-line and are packaged as teleclasses.

I personally have been conducting teleclasses since 2001 as a marketing tool as well as a product I offer for sale. It's an excellent way to get my message across to many more people, rather than relay my information to one person at a time... It has been a very lucrative profit center for me as well! I now interact with people from all over the world and provide value to each and every one of them.

I recommend you set up a series of teleclasses on a regular basis to let people "preview" your products and services and get to know you better. I offer them to my subscriber base with a link in my shopping cart. People register directly from the sign up link I send out or else go to my website and sign up. I use teleclasses as an educational tool, and as I promote myself I offer them for free on many occasions.

I also offer more advanced teleclasses as a product people can purchase and participate in. These are either one-time events or organized into an ongoing series of support calls. Content is determined by what best supports your target market. Some service providers may have a challenge changing from working privately and confidentially with an individual client to interacting with a group. I've discovered how the group dynamic adds another great element of support to the work I do with an individual. A wonderful benefit from the group work is the palpable energy created by having people live on the phone interacting with you as the expert, surrounded by a network of people learning from you and valuing your work. It's very fulfilling and it provides a valuable service to people who otherwise wouldn't get to experience you. Don't worry about compromising your integrity as you migrate from individual client contact as there are good ways to protect your integrity in a group scenario.

How do you create and offer a teleclass? There are many services available, and feel free try ones that appeal to you. Some are paid services, many are free.

One of the free services I recommend is www. nocostconference.com. You have more feature control with this service than with other free conference services out there. For this account, be sure to sign up for "web access" to be able to create and download recordings of your calls.

With your free account, you get a free dedicated number, a pin number for participants and a moderator code for yourself. Another feature I like is the ability to turn off sound effects, such as the beep when people enter and leave the call. You can also mute and unmute the group at will.

I believe that *everyone* should incorporate teleclass technology into whatever they're doing. It's so important, and it's easy to do. Do you have a coaching program and currently work one-on-one with your clients? You could package your coaching services. Rather than paying a higher one-on-one fee, your clients has another price option to join your group coaching. I *highly recommend* teleclasses! See www.intentionalincome.com for all the resources I recommend.

3. Special Report

A special report is a mini E-Book offered as a digital download item, rather than a physical product. You may have some content already or want to share other information from your business or industry. Perhaps you've written a curriculum manual, a how-to workbook or have "secret strategies" to share.

Creating a Special Report is a great way to repurpose content. Provide anywhere from 2-20 pages of content on any topic related to your industry. Maybe it's an article you've written or a piece someone else has written for you that you repackage with their permission.

Let people experience you in a different way before they are fully committed to working with you or purchasing products that cost more. For formatting instructions, refer to the E-Book section.

Special Reports are often used as a marketing tool and offered as a free gift or bonus, such as with a purchase, just as you received this E-Book with your purchase. There are other Special Reports I sell if people are receiving valuable information that I believe is worth a few dollars.

Take some time to consider what you do, your skills, talents, services, as I suggested earlier. What are you offering people? Who is your target market? List some interesting content for your niche. For example, in creating our funnel at www.cityscarves.com, our research revealed that women who buy scarves want to learn how to *wear* scarves. (That's actually a very heavily searched keyword phrase on the search engines.)

To meet this need, I created a Special Report on how to tie scarves. When people visit the website to look at our scarves, they feel compelled to sign in to get their free report. At this point they're in my funnel, and I can communicate to them about other product offerings on a regular basis.

4. E-Book

Any service provider, and just about any business, can create an E-Book to educate people and provide value around what they offer. E-books, which are electronic books in PDF format, are both very popular and very easy to create.

Once completed, E-Books can be sold over and over again with virtually no added effort. They are also a very lucrative market. They provide a great way to promote your products and services while providing value to people who want information on demand. I *highly* recommend E-Books as a marketing tool and a profit center in your business!

E-Books are created from Word documents converted to Adobe PDF format and uploaded to your shopping cart for full automation. You sell the final product through your website or link it to other sites. Your content can't be deleted or manipulated by the end user once it's produced, which protects your content, including your live links.

I buy E-Book s all the time to have instant access to information I need and save time over going to a bookstore or waiting for an Amazon order. The Adobe PDF format lets you provide not just live links, but also diagrams, and link them to other places, including your website. An E-book is somewhat interactive, as compared to a traditional book.

Another secret I want to share on how to produce content *much faster* is to record the content first, using your conference call service, and then have the files transcribed into written word for editing. I do this all the time and it's great! You can also use voice activated software that transcribes as you talk, such as Naturally Speaking from Dragon Software. See my other recommended resources at www. intentionalincome.com to help you with the mechanics of creating an E-Book .

5. Audio products

Audio products are easy to make and can be combined with your E-Books or sold stand alone. You can create a first rate audio program in a recording studio and with professionally editing, as I used to do.

However, there are many options these days. Today you can literally record in front of a computer, as I often do. We have a little recording studio in our house with a professional grade Snowball microphone and editing software. Make your own audio programs this way if you or someone you know understands editing software programs such as GarageBand or Sound Forge.

Another way to record an audio program is to create live programs and record your programs for a more dynamic interactive effect. The least expensive option I have found is to use the free telephone conference call service with the recording features I mentioned earlier. When complete with your call, download the audio file into your computer for later editing, including adding music or other content. It's a very inexpensive way to create an audio program that could ultimately be sold as a product. Local sound and video recording resources are in the phonebook or on www.craigslist.org .and check out www.audioacrobat.com as another vehicle to create audio products.

Audio programs were historically sold as CD sets and kits that you buy online or in stores. The physical program used to have a higher perceived value than purchasing a book. These days, you don't even have to have the physical products. Today's technology lets us upload our digital, or electronic, files to websites and direct customers to a digital file for direct download to their iPod or computer, where they can burn their own CDs if they choose.

It's a terrific way to get your message out there. Your on-demand digital product requires no maintenance and has little cost to produce. In my Passion To Prosperity Protégé Program (www.passion2prosperity.com), I create an audio product for each of my clients to sell online or at events.

6. Video products

Many people have very visual products they could create, especially if there's something in the business that features a specific technology or application. Is there a type of training you do, or something with high visual appeal? A video program is a wonderful way to duplicate yourself and serve more people.

Once you create your video program, the supply is endless. I recommend professional grade video edited by a professional videographer, who can also add music and other effects to the final product. I highly recommend the investment. We live in a very multi-sensory, visual world and I believe *everyone* in business should be working with video on some level.

These days it's also very easy to produce your own videos, however. New technology, including editing software, lends itself to the do-it-yourselfers. Try using a Flip Video camera (www.theflip.com) for simple do-it-yourself projects. Someone can help you edit and add effects and music.

Your video programs can be used as a marketing tool on your website and offered for free to help build your funnel or even put on www.YouTube. com, or become a profit center and sold as a package online and offline.

7. Coaching/consulting packages

Anyone can create their own individual consulting and coaching around their core talent. Many people do that very successfully, but the goal should be to ultimately *stop* trading your time for dollars. Realize how valuable your time is, and that you have the opportunity to create other products and services.

This may be a paradigm shift for you, but let me emphasize that one-on-one coaching or consulting services should be your premium item, for which you charge a premium fee. You can have packages at varying price points, including a basic group coaching package up to and including a premium one-on-one package that lasts for an extended period of time, or until a certain goal is accomplished. I created several packages that I offer to my prospective clients ---- group coaching teleclasses starting at $50/month, monthly coaching for $500, 3 month consulting packages for $5000, and a $10,000 consulting package.

8. Your idea as an invention

Is there an aspect of your talent or an idea that can become an invention? Have you created tools to help provide your service? Create intellectual property, such as a patent or a trademark. I've gone down this path, and while it requires intense focus and busy days for a period of time, the rewards of developing an invention are not only financial but personal as well. You might find to wise to sell your company, merge with another, do an Initial Public Offering, (IPO) or get paid to step back and allow others to run it.

Your IP could become a tangible product, a "widget" that you patent and sell. It could even be a business process that you patent, since business processes --- how you do things --- are patentable. Go to www.uspto.gov to see if your idea has been patented already. Alternatively, work with Intellectual Property or Patent attorneys to conduct the search and file the patents.

Once your protection is in place, there are people who want to invest money to help you develop the idea. With the proper resources and team, you can outsource the manufacturing of your invention and ultimately see your products sold in stores like Wal-Mart or the stores where you want to sell them sold. There are several resources available for people who want to develop ideas and raise capital. I've listed my favorite ones at www.intentionalincome. com . Think about how your talents or skills can transform into a patentable product and start listing your ideas!

9. Publish a book

We all have a book inside us! I highly recommend packaging your talents and skills into a book. Is there an aspect of your services to package as a how-to, a tell-all that dispels a myth, a compilation series, or perhaps you want to write the story of your journey? Maybe there's something you do that is highly illustrative--- *put it in a book.*

A book these days is not only a profit center--- it's also a calling card for use as a marketing tool. If you go the traditional route of having a book published by a large publishing house, work with a literary agent who submits for you. There are also a number of self-publishing and print-on-demand resources, such as www.iuniverse.com or Amazon's www.booksurge.com to get your book out there faster and realize more of the profits for yourself. Ghost writers and editors are readily available from online freelance jobsites such as www.elance.com or www.craigslist.org.

10. Workshops

I recommend incorporating workshops into your service offerings. Workshops are smaller, more interactive versions of seminars, and a great way to showcase your talents, introduce participants to other good resources, and potentially create substantial revenue for yourself. There are many inexpensive venue options for workshops and you can pre-sell admission for an instant source of revenue.

11. Seminars

Seminars are a format typically for larger groups and delivered in a lecture style with less participation from the attendees. I highly recommend developing a workshop or a seminar around what you're doing. It could be an event where you're the primary speaker, or primary talent. It could be a collaborative event, where you bring other resources in to support your potential customers.

Workshops and seminars are either free or paid events. Short events are used more as a preview for a bigger premium priced product or service that you're promoting or they can be a profit center unto themselves.

12. E-Learning modules or mini-courses

I highly recommend considering the talents and skills that you possess, or whatever you're sharing with other people, and creating E-learning materials and mini-courses. Break your content up into small modules and make them available online as a course with downloadable material.

Once a week, once a month, or maybe once a day your customers get their lessons. Stretch your course out over a period of time with a lot of value built into it if you want. You can give away modules or courses as a gift to let people experience you for a time before they actually engage you, or this could definitely be a new profit center for you. They are easy to create as a digital product (possibly just sending an email) and easy to automate with the proper autoresponder tools found at www.intentionalincome.com .

13. Subscriber lists for profit

In the later marketing section, I discuss list building as a primary activity for your business, to both increase your visibility and to draw more people into your funnel. Many of the products and services I discuss can be give-aways when people enter your funnel to provide a compelling reason to sign in, leave their email or contact information, and then receive ongoing communication from you.

Use your subscriber list as a profit center! That's why I include it here. In fact, with some people, their primary goal is to build large subscriber databases to promote other products and services for profit, charge classified advertising fees, or sell compiled data to third parties. If you're a connector or a great networker, this path could be a lucrative one for you. I include it in the marketing section, and also here in the product section as a recommended revenue stream.

14. Print newsletter

In addition to an ezine, consider a print newsletter. Print newsletters were in fashion years ago before the advent of electronic communication. However, they've recently come *back* in fashion as a great marketing tool. Many organizations today also offer print newsletters for a fee. Your choice could be to give away a print newsletter, or offer a fee based subscription.

15. Newspaper or magazine column

A newspaper or magazine column lets you easily share your talents with others. (This is in the marketing section because it's a great way to build awareness about what you're doing.) For this products and service section, realize that it's a potential profit center, especially as your column becomes *syndicated* to multiple media outlets.

16. Magazine or newspaper

I know several people that have started their own magazine or newspaper. They were service providers, who evolved into information product specialists, and now use the magazine to showcase their talent and the talents of their associates. Some had a hobby they loved and started a magazine to become more engaged in their "hobby". There are multiple revenue streams available to you on this path.

17. Membership based program

Offering continuity programs, or memberships, is very popular right now. You create wealth with the cumulative effect of passive revenue. Many businesses now include offline as well as online memberships in their product offerings. This is an excellent way to create recurring revenue in your business.

Provide a service to someone who benefits from it one time or over a period of time. When the services are complete, offer them a membership or affinity program so they continue experiencing you, perhaps at a reduced rate.

I currently offer a monthly membership program to my business start-up clients after they've completed my program at www.passion2prosperity.com . It's a great way for people to connect with an expert without paying high consulting fees. It also provides residual recurring revenue to my company.

Start your own membership website that is completely automated and user driven. Check out the resources available for this at www.intentionalincome.com .

18. Service retainers

Service retainers are similar to the membership program concept, but more of an "insurance policy" for someone who needs your services less frequently. It's another profit center of recurring revenue to offer clients after a primary service is complete.

19. Hosted networking groups or roundtables

This is a wonderful way to build alliances, to collaborate, and to bring people together. You not only get to share your talents with multiple people, but to create a profit center around things you love to do. Networking groups, Mastermind groups, and Roundtables are very popular, especially within specific target markets.

I highly recommend this as a profit center if you're in the business of connecting with the community. You're actually bringing the community together as you establish your own credibility. Consider yearly fees or fees based on usage.

20. Expo and trade show organization

At expos and trade shows you showcase your products and services, as well as those of your peers. Just like the networking groups, large groups of people come together to experience you, collaborate with others, and experience the multiple profit centers built into a trade show.

You don't have to do any of these alone. There are many people out there willing to collaborate

if they also have the opportunity to promote
THEIR business. Professional event planners are
very good to help you organize your expo or
trade show.

21. Screensavers

If you have something that's highly visual, or
messages that you would like to get out to
people on a regular basis, I recommend creating
your own screensavers. These are images that
float by on someone's computer during periods
of user inactivity. It's a downloadable digital
product you have made for you or else you
buy the software yourself. Once created, its
functionality is automated.

22. Warranty programs

There are warranty programs for high ticket
items, such as electronics and home appliances.
Replacement for breakdown is often costly.
It may be more economical to pay a small
monthly, or yearly, fee to cover replacement in
the event something goes wrong. If somebody
receives a service from you and they want to
ensure they won't have to pay the same fees
again, offer a warranty program if your business
allows for that. This can be a great source of
recurring revenue in your company.

23. Webinars

They are very similar to teleclasses, except they
take place online. People have the opportunity
to listen to you and watch a live instruction
online. This is preferable to a teleclass when you

want to teach a *visual lesson*. They are a very popular instruction method nowadays, and there are several webinar services available, such as www.gotowebinar.com, in addition to resources at www.intentionalincome.com .

24. Affiliate marketing

One of the fastest ways to create instant revenue is to promote and sell the products and services of others as an online affiliate. When you become an affiliate for a specific product or program, you get a specific link that tracks a prospect's activity on the website you're promoting. There's no inventory for you to manage or accounting details to handle, and you are paid whenever a purchase is made. Typical commissions average between 10% to 100% of the purchase price of the product.

This is much easier if you have a specific target market you're working with and you're actively building a subscriber list. For example, if you're doing anything related to stress reduction, products such as soothing lotions, meditation CDs, or other stress reducers fit this market. Rather than go out and invent or create these things on your own, simply become an affiliate for existing product companies.

Check out the websites of companies that sell products and services you resonate with and see if they have an affiliate program.

I officially invite you to become an affiliate of my programs by clicking on the affiliate link at www.mariasimone.com. You'll get instructions on how to use your links and promote my programs as soon as you sign in. You can also go to www.clickbank.com, which is an online marketplace offering thousands of affiliate opportunities for you to choose.

25. Network marketing

This is another form of affiliate marketing. You are independently selling the products or services of another company for a commission. Network Marketing (or Multi-Level Marketing) not only allows individuals to earn commissions from their sales, but also enroll others to promote and sell products as well, thereby earning you additional passive, or residual, commission. The people selling under you is called your downline.

Your long term financial success often depends on how successful you are in recruiting others to work with you. There are thousands of network marketing opportunities available across multiple industries sectors, such as health and fitness, business services, finance, and education. I encourage you to research an opportunity that would complement your existing lifestyle. You can find these opportunities through simple online searches. Be sure and investigate the validity of the opportunity, stability of the company, the compensation model, and make sure there is integrity with the products and services being promoted.

26. Licensing ideas

You may own the intellectual property rights to certain ideas, inventions and business systems that other companies would benefit from selling, or may need for their own purposes. License out or "rent" your technology and receive paid royalties. This is a great means of getting your products and services out there without spending much time and money developing them or incurring marketing expenses.

You can not only develop it for yourself, but also license your idea to other companies to receive royalties (similar to "rent") for the use of a product or service. Years ago I invented a novelty product and licensed the concept to an aromatherapy company in California. They developed, manufactured and sold my product idea and I collected royalty checks every quarter.

Royalties paid for licensed properties average between 3%- 20% of net sales and include art, software inventions, electronics, and so on. Hire a licensing agent to work with you, or do the research on your own of companies that might be interested in your ideas.

27. Software utility (or version) based on what you do

Is there something you do that you could create a software program around to automate a function? Could you create a special-purpose calculator or measurement tool for visitors?

This was done by my friend Burke Franklin, the founder of Jian. He created BizPlan Builder, which has become one of the top selling electronic business planning tools. He also automated the sales plan and marketing plan process, and created downloadable contracts and stock options. Check out his programs at www.manifestsuccessplanning.com .

28. Games

A great way to package your talent is to create a game for entertainment or educational purposes. Is there some instruction set you could package as an educational tool or a game? Facts you have to share? It could be a fun way to provide training or used as a communication tool. There are games related to wealth creation, relationship building, safety issues, and cooking.

29. "Train the Trainer" program

If the service you provide can be systematized and ultimately duplicated, consider creating a program to teach others how to deliver your service. It could be a facilitator training program. That's a great way to serve more people, because now you're really teaching people to "do what you do" as a profit center. Thereafter, if they go out and teach your curriculum, they will pay you a licensing fee, or royalty, for the use of your program or for your materials. People such as John Gray, Tony Robbins and Robert Kiyosaki all teach their methods to others for a fee and ongoing royalties thereafter.

30. Deck of cards

A deck of cards could be inspirational or educational in nature or just for fun. It's a profitable way to repurpose content you have, or information you share on a regular basis with your customers. Check out one resource at www. mem-cards.com .

31. Advertising on your website

An easy way to monetize your website or blog is to sell advertising space or monetize with Google Adsense. This is an automated way to bring in other service providers and advertisers that cater to your market.

Sign up with Google for a free Adsense account at adsense.google.com. Load the banner onto your website or blog, and the Google ads automatically appear on your website. You are compensated when people click through the links appearing on your site. Millions of people utilize this service to create substantial online revenue. It may or may not be right for you. As you build your traffic rankings---the number of visitors to your site-- offer a more sophisticated advertising opportunity for others who will pay you to have their ads on your website or blog. Work with a blog advertising specialist such as you find at www.blogads.com .

32. Self-improvement CD

If you're in the business of helping people improve their lives, and live their magnificence, then it is great to provide them inspirational tools that reinforce your message, such as a meditation CD, or allow them to continue the work that they've done with you in private.

33. Art work for your business

Is there any aspect of your business that could be illustrated graphically and sold as prints or developed into products for profit? That's something to think about. Artists from all over the country have created art for me that was rendered into *City Scarves* and then sold in department stores and gift shops. Once the art is created, use it over and over again on multiple products.

34. Novelty items

Expand your brand to promotional items as another product offering. Products can include t-shirts, mugs, computer accessories, and so on. See my most updated promotional resources at www.intentionalincome.com .

35. Reselling

This is the offline version of affiliate marketing. You create the opportunity to sell the products and services of other companies to your target market instead of developing your own. It's a *much faster* way to develop revenue. You can also "private label" products made by other companies and put your name on it.

Trader Joe's is one of my favorite grocery stores and I love the variety of health conscious foods they offer. All their products carry the Trader Joe's name yet *none* are made by Trader Joe's. The company private labels food products that are manufactured by other companies.

36. Brokering deals

This is great if you're naturally a networker or connecter and tend to meet a lot of people. There are always people who need things to match up with people who have something to offer. When you put people together who otherwise wouldn't have met, you are entitled to compensation if there is a financial gain in the relationship.

I do this on a regular basis and I teach others how to do it in my coaching programs. People come to me all the time looking for certain resources. If I can find that particular resource for them, I should get compensated for making the connection.

For example, I recently met someone who manufactures musical collectibles and distributes them to department stores all over the country. I happened to also know someone who invented a new type of collectible and had a patent on it. I asked the manufacturer if he was interested in introducing some new technology into his company and he said yes. I brought them together and they'll probably be working together going forward--- he'll manufacture and distribute her item through a licensing agreement and she'll collect royalties The person who is getting paid, the inventor in this case, is going to benefit financially and she's more than happy to give me a percentage of her royalties because I put the deal together.

If you're a networker by nature, or attract people who are constantly looking for different products or resources for their life or their business, be intentional about making connections and benefiting financially from them. Ask for a fee or a royalty, preferably an ongoing residual fee for the work you do to put the deal together. You need to be very intentional about it and speak up early on. Put some of the terms together up front if there's room for this kind of negotiation.

Most of the time we do things just to help other people and don't expect compensation --- you are still doing everyone a great service by making the connection AND you have every right to ask for compensation. Connections can be for new business for which you should receive a percentage or a referral fee, investor capital for a percentage of the money raised, contacts for manufacturing or other business resources.

37. Kit or bundled offer

Are you currently selling different products and services individually, or know other people with products and services that would meet your customer's needs as well? By bundling them together in an offer, you benefit even more financially, because you are either selling more items to your customer, or the novelty effect produces a bigger demand. That's another profit center in your business – create a kit or bundled offer of complementary products and services.

38. Blogs

Years ago, not everyone had a website, but today you're not even considered a credible business if you don't. Blogs are very popular these days and it's now expected that everyone has a blog. Most people use blogs to communicate with their potential market or to journal what's happening in their life.

A blog is a very interactive tool you can monetize through advertising and memberships. Blog popularity increases the more specific it is to a particular topic or serves a specific market segment. Google's free blog service is at www.blogger.com and there's also www.wordpress.com and www.typepad.com . You can sign up for Google Adsense and bring in a service like www.blogads.com to help monetize with advertising revenue.

39. Franchising your business

Franchising can be an excellent way to expand your product and service offerings without you doing all the work.

If you're a service business and been successful in business and profitable for six months or more, you may have an opportunity to franchise. If you're in retail with an existing retail space, or you have real estate attached to your business and you've been profitable for at least two years, you may have a franchise opportunity. A franchise team comes in and helps you package everything unique to your business – all the systems, the way you provide your services, all your operations --- and sell it to franchisees that duplicate your system and pay you franchise fees.

Not only can you make hundreds of thousands of dollars selling a good franchise, but thereafter, you collect franchise fees. That's a great way to bring more profit into your business without you doing all the work. One of my colleagues is Frank Flack, who founded the very successful Molly Maid franchise. He taught me a lot about the power of franchising and how it can help small business owners have explosive growth.

40. Radio or podcast hosting

Another exciting way for you to serve more people and get your message out there is to host your own radio or podcast program. A podcast is similar to a radio interview but it's a pre-recorded segment you post online at places like www. iTunes.com or on your website for listeners to check in at a later time.

Having a presence on the airwaves is, of course, for marketing and PR purposes, while also creating a profit center when you add in advertisers and paying guests. By hosting your own radio or podcast program, you literally create multiple profit centers as well as have a new way to promote your own programs.

There are internet based programs, such as www.blogtalkradio.com and I list a number of resources for you at www.intentionalincome.com.

41. TV program hosting

In the same way you benefit financially from a radio program, those mechanisms and more are built into having your own TV show even though more planning and financial resources are needed. TV programs are hosted on websites as well, such as the popular edutainment site http://tv.winelibrary.com/.

42. Plays

Creating a play around your talents, to tell your story or share a lesson, is an interesting profit center for you when you consider the additional merchandising revenue. I knew someone who succeeded at this a couple of years ago. She wrote a book based on stories about mothers and daughters which was published and did very well. She took it to another level by bringing the book to life on the stage. It's taking off as I write this and it's amazing to watch her progress. Is there something you're doing that would be better expressed as a play?

43. Checklists, forms or templates

Create a series of lists and templates that people can access for a fee and download to help automate their tasks. People will pay for any information that saves them time or money or increases their productivity.

44. Statistics and resource lists

Compile information from various sources that people download for a fee. This can be applied to any industry including fashion, real estate, lifestyle, health, wellness, career, finance, etc.

When I'm researching for a book or working on a project and want a list of resources, I have frequently bought the information online so I could receive already compiled info. This does not have to be complicated. In fact, simplicity is best and easier to promote than something too complicated!

45. Announcement Alerts

Charge a fee for access to timely information you share with others. I subscribe to several services that provide me with business info, health and fashion alerts. One of my favorites is an alert I get several times a week that lets me know what political legislation issues are active involving women's rights.

Believe it or not, we're just getting started even though it's the end of this section! I have given you 44 sample ways to create products and services around your existing talents, skills, and passions.

If you're in business currently providing a service, look at how to incorporate some of these into your existing business as additional profit centers. If you are in transition and you're just now tapping into your passion, consider promoting other people's products and services that pique your interest or look at connecting people for profit.

If you're just starting out, and wondering how to express your talents, this section revealed some real, tried-and-true methods. Pick a few that are right for you at this time. Pick ones that resonate with your lifestyle and most benefit your target market. It's an excellent way to start packaging your talents and you'll build from there.

All of these products and services are interchangeable. Some will be used as marketing tools or as value added services that you give away. You'll find you can monetize *all* of these to provide different levels of service. *It's so exciting!* I wanted to plant the seeds here for you in this E-Book. Read on for more valuable tips!

⌘ ⌘ ⌘

Formulate and stamp indelibly on your mind a mental picture of yourself as succeeding. Hold this picture tenaciously. Never permit it to fade. Your mind will seek to develop the picture...Do not build up obstacles in your imagination.

~~~Norman Vincent Peale

VIII. CHAPTER EIGHT ~ ATTRACT CUSTOMERS WITH EASE

A. Distinctions between SALES, MARKETING and PR

Marketing is one of my favorite activities in any business I work on! In my *Passion To Prosperity Protégé Program*, I spend a lot of time showing people how to make a name for themselves as they automate these strategies. Before I continue, it's important to make some distinctions between the role sales, marketing, and PR play in your business.

1. "PR" or public relations/ publicity

PR is all about creating a buzz about you and your company. The buzz may have *nothing* directly to do with your product or your company! It's a way to tell your story and draw interest. You announce an activity or event, something that's taking place in your company, a change, such as a new affiliation.

It may be something outrageous to get people talking about you. A while back, I saw a news story about someone auctioning a grilled cheese sandwich on eBay. The sandwich appeared to have the image of the Madonna in the middle of it. A *bidding war* took place for the sandwich, which happened to be several years old by the time! (This was *not* a fresh sandwich!)

In any event, the winning bidder was an online poker website. The name of the company traveled all over the place. Even CNN gave the story airtime. The publicity they received was priceless, and even though the event had nothing to do with their company, they became known to many millions of people. That's just one illustration of how someone created a buzz. It's important to have some type of publicity effort happening in your company on a regular basis. Regularly issue press releases at the very least.

2. The sales function in your business is very important.

This is where someone is designated to write the order, make a transaction and actually exchange money for goods and services. There should be an ongoing sales effort taking place in your business. Somebody either needs to be out there in your business completing transactions for you, or prospective customers have to complete the sales transaction themselves when they call you directly or get online.

It takes up to seven impressions to get a sale. We may be introduced to a product or service once or twice, and it may not make any impression on us at first. Years ago it only took two or three impressions to result in a sale of a product or service. But these days, since we're so bombarded with messages from advertising media and have so much visual stimulation around us, we have to be introduced and reintroduced to a product or service seven times before we follow through with a buying decision.

Remember this when you're creating your funnel and promoting your products!

3. Marketing is building awareness about your products

Usually there's some education involved in this function. It's an integral and continuous process if you use the marketing funnel techniques discussed earlier. Sometimes the sales function is combined with marketing. It can be systematized in your company and automated. It's also takes place where you're building a relationship with potential customers as you provide value and education.

My company, Signature Accents, produces a line of *City Scarves*, as I mentioned. One of the marketing programs is a program called "Fit To Be Tied". We send out teams to department stores to participate in scarf tying events in the accessory departments. There are mailings to customers ahead of time, as well as press releases and announcements in the local paper. We invite customers into the store to come to the scarf counter for a free scarf tying event. It's a purely educational event yet usually as a result of receiving education about tying scarves, the customer buys one of our scarves. That's only one of the ways we market to our customers and the ultimate result is actually the sale of a scarf or two. In this section the focus is on marketing but remember that it's best to have a continuous PR, sales and marketing program in place in your company.

B. The Purpose of your Marketing Campaign

For whom and when can these techniques be used? Initially in your campaign, use marketing to build your subscriber base and support your sales effort, as discussed earlier. One of the things to set up in your organization is a sales funnel. The wide end is where people are first introduced to your company, products and services. The narrow end is where pre-qualified individuals are making buying decisions for your premium products and services.

Once we build your funnel and have an array of products and services lining it, you'll use various techniques to introduce customers to your offerings. Having a subscriber base to interact with on a regular basis translates into sales. Remember, it takes up to seven impressions for people to make a buying decision. Your marketing campaign drives potential customers into your funnel so they start experiencing you on many different levels. *Build that list!*

You can start offering your subscribers free products, services and subscriptions. You will also be introducing them to educational content or at least sharing the benefits of what you offer, such as more money, happier kids, whiter teeth, fulfilling career, and so on. Remember, you've invited these people to enter your world by subscribing to your database, and they've accepted the invitation. They're *expecting you* to communicate with them!

Any individual who wants to increase their exposure on search engines and in the media for branding purposes must have a marketing program in place. Put yourself out there and reach the masses. It's also important that people are able to find you with search engines such as Google and Yahoo when they type in your name and your product or service. Intentionally create that visibility for yourself and institute a marketing program that helps maintain a high level of visibility and awareness. It may not even be for you personally, but awareness should be created for what you offer.

All of my projects have an active marketing campaign in place. When I'm launching a new program or book, I can achieve success more quickly and easily, because I've already built the demand for it ahead of time.

C. 45 Potential Marketing Techniques You Can Implement

1. A website as a marketing tool

Having a presence online is like having a business card these days. It's not absolutely necessary, yet if you don't have it, you'll spend a lot more time personally communicating your information to people, and you may not be taken as seriously. If you don't have your own website, make sure the programs you offer have an online connection, regardless of your industry. A website is one of the most cost-effective marketing tools you can have.

There are many ways to get a website done, but if you're on a tight budget start by registering a domain name at www.snagadomain.com (a subsidiary of GoDaddy) for just a few dollars and then order one of their template based websites. An inexpensive blogging service that looks good enough to use as a website can be found at Typepad.com. My husband, Michael Murdock, can also provide you with affordable solutions at www.docmurdock.com and you'll find other resources at www.intentionalincome.com .

2. A blog as a marketing tool

I highly recommend having a blog, as they are very popular and rank high in visibility with search engines. A blog is a communication tool, like an online journal that connects you with the public. You don't have as much artistic control as you would have on a website, but it's an excellent way to get your message out, as it tends to be more conversational in nature. There are several free blog services, such as www.blogger.com and www.wordpress.com

3. Circulate your ezine

Previously we discussed an ezine as a product offering; it is also an excellent marketing tool. I recommend offering a complimentary subscription to anyone you meet or who visits your website, as a means for them to experience you on many levels.

4. Offer a bonus gift to other programs

This is a great way to market your products and services. Offer a free product to the customers of a colleague. You may have the products and services----someone else may have the subscriber base you desire. It is worth it for you to collaborate in this way, as your colleague's customers ultimately become yours'.

My *Passion To Prosperity Protégé Program* is a 6-figure business building program for small businesses. I collaborate with wealth managers and business credit line experts who offer free bonus gifts to my subscribers since business building, financing and wealth management go hand in hand. By the same token, I offer free bonus gifts about business building to their customers. Sharing information with our respective customer lists helps each of us grow our businesses very passively and effortlessly. Your bonus gift could be a digital information product or a tangible gift.

5. Offer a gift with purchase

This is very similar to #4. If you want people to sample a product of yours so they can decide if they want to purchase it, offer a free sample of it when they purchase another product from you. This includes trial memberships as well.

6. Article submission

A great way to increase your online traffic and get exposure is to submit short articles to free article content submission sites. I love to write, and find I have great results with the article sites I currently use.

There are many people publishing newspapers and magazines, online ezines, and offline newsletters. They are looking for content for their periodicals and get it from the many free article submission sites on the Internet. Once you submit your content, you are picked up by those LOOKING for content.

Some of my favorites are www.ideamarketers. com and www.eZineArticles.com. Simply set up free accounts and submit articles averaging 500 words. If you get adventurous, submit to hundreds of sites. You'll find automated article submitter software at www.intentionalincome. com.

In my Protégé program, I show clients how to generate money-making content. I encourage people to develop content that best highlights your product or service. The purpose is not to sell it, but rather to educate people on the benefits of what you offer. You'll get full credit with your name, bio, and website links. Once you submit the article to these sites, they maintain the integrity of your contact info within your article. People who read and syndicate your articles will maintain your name, your website, and all of your links. Once again, it's a fabulous way to get exposure for what you do, and it's all free. I have written dozens and dozens of articles that have been picked up by other services. They continue to populate the search engines and drive traffic to my websites.

7. Participate in online discussion groups

 This is very easy to do and is a free service at www.YahooGroups.com or www.GoogleGroups.com. Pick a topic in an industry for which you feel an affinity, and join one of the many thousands of groups discussing that topic. You can even start your own discussion group. I joined some of the groups related to inventors, start-up businesses, women in business, fashion designers and so forth.

There are all kinds of discussion groups, ranging from lifestyle to health, finance and business. Your email goes out to the entire group, and individuals can respond directly to you thereafter. Discussion groups are not typically meant for selling---be sure to join the discussion group that looks interesting and watch the dialog that is taking place to understand the nuance of the group before you jump in and start sending emails. Each of them has different rules of how to engage in conversation. It can be a great marketing tool for you as you share your talents with members of the discussion group.

8. Lead generation with TrafficSwarm

This is one of the many traffic generation websites out there. For a free account, go to www.trafficswarm.com . Basically you get to submit your website link and a little description of your website that potentially goes out to hundreds of thousands of visitors. You click on other links to get credit and the more credit you accumulate, the more your site gets promoted. You can buy credits as well for more exposure. It's an interesting tool and really does generate traffic to your website. I recommend establishing an account.

9. Establish a presence on social networking sites

Online social networking sites are very popular right now. If you're not involved in at least one social networking group, such as www.Facebook.com , I highly recommend you start. Social networking lets you tap into an online community in open dialog to share your thoughts, your talents, and to build relationships. Two sites that are more business oriented, but not as dynamic as Facebook, are www.Fastpitchnetworking.com and www.LinkedIn.com .

10. Search Engine Optimization (SEO)

SEO includes keyword submission of your site and many activities related to raising your visibility with the search engines. That's why you embed metatags, or certain key words, in your website content. Then you submit your site to search engines like Google, Yahoo and MSN to get picked up during their site indexing process. If people 'Google' your name, product, service, or anything related to you--- you want your website to show up and potential customers to find you.

If your website isn't optimized properly, it's more difficult to generate traffic from people looking for what you offer. They'll never find you. You can do some of this preparation on your own, but it really helps to work with a professional. For more information and SEO service offerings go to www.docmurdock.com

11. Submit press releases

Press releases have historically been categorized as publicity, yet more and more people now use press releases as a marketing tool. I include press releases in this section as a reminder for you to get on a regular submission schedule of press releases. In the past people wrote the press release and then faxed it to newspapers and other media outlets. This was very tedious Most of the process is now automated.

More and more press release services have sprung up online to make things easier. You sign up for an account and then upload your press release, which goes out to hundreds of outlets. www.l-newswire.com and www.PRlog.org are two free press release submission services. There is also www.PRweb.com and www.PRnewswire. com . I have press release submission services through my account at FastPitch Networking,

I recommend staying in touch more personally with your local media, even as you utilize the online services, as it is easier to get exposure on a local level.

12. Create reciprocal links with other websites

This is a terrific way to increase exposure for your products and services, and to get higher rankings on the search engines. Of course be very responsible and make sure that the links you're reciprocating with belong to reputable businesses that provide complementary services to your target market. It's another form of online collaboration and a great way to get your message out there.

13. Post regularly on www.Craigslist.org

Craigslist is a wonderful free community bulletin board where you can post free events, product and service offerings, as well as seek opportunities for joint collaborations

14. Utilize Google Adwords --- "Pay Per Click"

Google Adwords is a pay per click situation. They are typically the paid advertisements you may see on the right side of the page after a Google search. You can set up a free account at adwords.google.com . It's free to create, but be warned that your costs with this service do add up.

Depending on the search topic, an appropriate ad will pop up to the right of your search findings, and when someone clicks the link, the person's account is charged for the "click". It's a great way to practically guarantee traffic and visibility, however remember to manage your account closely and establish a budget!

15. Email blasts

For instant gratification online, you can purchase email lists that many thousands of people have opted-into and given permission to be marketed to on various topics. These are compiled and sold by different companies. Do your due diligence on the companies selling the lists and the best way to promote your information. Not all of them are reputable! Make sure you have a very "clean" list.

You can research online about email blasters and purchasing lists. This would NOT be my primary marketing choice when I'm starting a campaign, but it is effective for certain products and services.

16. Print Newsletters

A print newsletter is a great marketing tool that can also serve as a profit center. Print newsletters were very popular years ago and they're coming back in fashion. You can even purchase pre-made newsletters and customize them with your information.

17. Group teleclasses

Another great marketing tool you can offer for free to "preview" some of your higher priced items is a group teleclass. Rather than you having individual conversations to educate people about the benefits of your products and services, it's best to have a teleclass to introduce your program to many people at the same time.

18. Get out there and speak

A powerful way to market your products and services is to let people experience you on a personal level, which you can easily accomplish through public speaking. There are many opportunities for you to go out there and share your talent. Paid speaking engagements are ideal and should be included as a profit center in your business, but it should not preclude you from offering your services for free, especially if you've done the work of creating additional products and services to offer your listeners.

Reach out to your local community based organizations, libraries, speaker's bureaus, Rotary Clubs, networking groups and churches. I "give to get" and frequently offer my services for free since I'll usually have the opportunity to promote my coaching programs during my presentation.

19. Promote videos on www.youtube.com

YouTube has proven to be a very popular video social networking site and since it's such a highly visual experience, I recommend uploading your own video clips onto your free account. Your videos could be you in action or may not have anything to do with your products and services.

Since millions of people every day watch the videos on YouTube, having any kind of presence potentially has a nice viral referral marketing effect in your business.

20. Become a guest on radio programs

It's not difficult to actually become a guest on a radio program. You simply have to be persistent and make sure your message is timed perfectly to what's relevant in the news.

I personally love to be interviewed and find this to be a very powerful marketing tool. The dynamics of two or more people in conversation are much more exciting than one person on a stage. It's a great way for you to get the word out to a larger audience about your products and services as you establish yourself as an expert on your topic of interest.

Start out with local stations as a regular talk radio guest and then branch out to more national and syndicated programs. Radio guests typically call in from the comfort of their home; they rarely go to the station. Being a guest is something you can do for free, from the comfort of your home, and reach millions of people. For my up-to-date resources go to www.intentionalincome.com One of my personal recommendations is Marsha Friedman at www.emsincorporated.com Her firm specializes in media bookings and her fees are the most affordable I've seen for this kind of service.

21. Get interviewed on TV

I highly recommend becoming a TV interview guest. to take the next step (for the same reasons listed in #20) and if you feel your product or service would translate well to TV. You can become an expert in your field, and put yourself out there as an available guest.

How do you become an expert in your field? Declare it to be the case, for starters! You can also establish yourself through your education, an accomplishment, your story, an experience, a book you've written on the subject, your track record, and so on.

22. Create Joint Ventures

I highly recommend collaborating with other businesses to market your products and services. This is an excellent way to market yourself and typically requires no upfront cost, yet the rewards of having a third party endorsement are tremendous. Go to people or businesses that cater to your target population and look at doing some online or offline promotion together. This could include an email announcement for a product launch, bundling products, or collaborating in some way so people start experiencing you as they buy the products and services of the other company.

This is such an important activity in any business, I devote an entire session to showing my clients how to create lucrative alliances in my *Passion To Prosperity Protégé Program*. Over the years, the alliances I've created with other professionals have produced hundreds of thousands of dollars in revenue for me, additional media attention, speaking engagements, and have also helped me build a very healthy subscriber list.

23. Conduct or participate in workshops

Workshops are great marketing tools as well as excellent profit centers if you choose to charge a fee. They can be educational, provide a valuable service to people, and be a great platform to promote your product offerings.

24. Offer a free consultation

Obviously it's important to manage your time spent on free consultations, but often people will make a purchase if they can experience you to a certain degree. Instead of only promoting your paid services, offer a free consultation and see how much more attention you get.

25. Public speaking

As I mentioned before, public speaking fits into the marketing category and can broadly include different formats, including panel discussions, debates and roundtable programs.

26. Exhibit at tradeshows

Exhibiting at tradeshows or even attending them, is a great way to market yourself. Include trade shows in your budget on a regular basis if you can and make sure you have a marketing funnel established for all attendees you meet. In fact, there are several businesses I know that utilize tradeshow activity as their primary point of contact for all potential customers. They attend two to three tradeshows a month and the revenues from the contacts they make at the shows represent the majority of their company sales.

27. Make in-store appearances

Are there locations where your products are being sold? Would you like to get connected to the customers of those retail stores? If so, organize personal appearances in those stores. Previously, I told you about our department store marketing program called "Fit to be Tied" where we go into department stores such as Bloomingdales and Macy's and host free scarf tying events. Showing up at the stores and being treated as a celebrity is a great way to establish yourself.

You may not have products being sold in stores but you should reach out to a certain customer base who shops at a particular store. One of my clients is a raw food chef who offers cooking demonstrations at her local healthy food markets. Not only is she getting paid for the in-store events, the people who attend the events become her customers and the media generated each time she speaks attracts more and more subscribers to her website. If this could be you, offer your services for an educational event tied to a holiday or a current event in the news.

28. Host a fundraiser or some type of charity-related event

Supporting a great cause is an excellent way for you to build relationships with your community, get the media involved in a good cause, and build lots of awareness about what you are doing. I put hosting a fundraiser as an actual marketing event because of the positive acclaim that will ensue as a result of you giving back. This is referred to as "cause-marketing."

29. Sponsor an event

You may not have the immediate resources to put on a trade show or a community event. You can still sponsor such events to support what's happening and get your name out there without committing yourself to coordinating the event yourself. Look at opportunities to sponsor an event, even if only means donating products or services for gift bags or auction items.

30. Direct mail campaign

Direct mail is one of the oldest, tried-and-true means of reaching potential customers. I highly recommend a mailing campaign with your existing or prospective customers. It should be a highly a coordinated event, with appropriate follow-up planned in advance. Besides the budget you'll require for an effective campaign, understand nuances such as what type of copy people respond to, best days for a mailing, and other factors.

31. Attend networking events

Just show up! This connects you with potential customers, educates the community, helps you establish potential Joint Venture relationships, and lets you market your products and services. Regular appearances should be incorporated into any type of marketing campaign. I recommend setting your intention ahead of time of what you want to create for yourself at each event so you have a more focused and productive effort. These events could be industry related business or for social networking--- anyplace where people gather to meet other like-minded individuals.

32. Host a contest or awards program

Hosting contests and awards program gains attention for what you're doing. I've done this frequently when I wanted feedback on something I was working on. It gave us a reason to reach out to the community, let them know what we're up to, and also offer opportunities for awards. Did you know there are many companies that will help sponsor your contest and offer prizes if you organize the event? The same is true for honoring another individual for their accomplishments or commitment to the community.

33. Conduct surveys

A great way to know what kind of products and services your potential customers want is to ask them. Talking to your potential customers is a marketing effort in and of itself. Just the fact that you're asking for feedback really elevates you in the eyes of your potential customers! There are free survey resources, such as www.surveymonkey.com that you can use for this activity.

34. Host a roundtable or panel event.

Hosting a roundtable or panel event brings members of your community together and provides educational value for prospective customers. Inviting several colleagues or industry experts to discuss certain issues also helps build awareness for what you're doing.

35. Host networking events

Many businesses organize their own networking events on a regular basis to not only have fun and reach out to the community, but to continually build awareness for their products and services. It helps you win allegiance from the community and from prospective customers. You can do it online or offline. If you use this as a marketing tool to support a bigger vision, make it a free event that attracts more attendees.

36. Facilitate no-host luncheons

Similar to a networking event is the no-host luncheon that is conducted around a meal, with or without a speaker involved. It's a great way to get people together very informally and inexpensively.

37. Put together a support group

Cater to a certain population that needs additional support apart from your primary service offerings. This could include those who are grieving, recovering from an addiction, living with a certain medical condition, and so on. Hosting and forming support groups is an excellent way for you to show up for your customers and elevate your standing in the community.

38. Volunteer your expertise as a mentor

I do this quite frequently for different organizations. What I give in time and compassion comes back to me in amazing ways! Besides the personal rewards of helping others, it's a fabulous way for you to get your name out there and build awareness for what you do. There are a variety of organizations both locally and nationally with their own mentor programs. Find one that's right for you or consider starting your own!

39. Bundle offers to existing customers

If you want to market a new product or service and have existing customers, consider bundling your new products and services with those they are currently buying from you. Let them try it for free for a short period of time, offer a coupon, or let them share a product with a friend. Whatever you feel is the best way to reach them will be the right choice.

40. Have others endorse you through their networks

Getting third party testimonials and praise are excellent ways to market yourself. When someone else sings your praises, it creates much more credibility for you. Actively seek endorsements from other people, especially within specific organizations. If you're really interested in tapping into a certain target market or demographic, find out who these people admire and emulate. Seek out the people who represent this population, and ask for their endorsement. Book authors do it all the time, and you've seen endorsements and testimonials on different publications that you read. It's a smart thing to do in any business!

41. Special bonus gift for referrals

Your customers are your greatest assets, so offer them something special when they refer to you. If you have an effective referral marketing campaign built into your business, your customers will literally grow your business for you. I know many who have spent zero dollars in advertising and publicity because they built in a terrific referral program with their existing customer base.

42. Frequent buyer rewards programs

Earlier I discussed one of the best ways to grow your business using a referral program with existing customers. Besides offering bonuses for referrals, I recommend another bonus program for those who frequently buy your products and services. Showing appreciation to customers inspires loyalty and motivates people to refer others to you. I believe that is one of the most effective marketing campaigns you could put in place in your business.

43. Post comments on blogs and other online resources

You will increase your online visibility by showing up and commenting on blogs, posting book reviews on Amazon.com, and other sites where comments are welcomed. This includes the online versions of newspapers and magazines.

44. Microblog on Twitter

Connect with others on www.Twitter.com. It's like Facebook on steroids! It may seem frivolous, yet millions of people use the service and there's lots of activity. Follow people who have large groups following them and connect to their followers as well. I've created a number of interesting collaborations from my activity on Twitter. Find me there!

45. Create a "lens" at Squidoo

www.Squidoo.com is a new way to get instant visibility to a large user group by creating a micro profile called a "lens" and then connecting with the larger group.

⌘ ⌘ ⌘

"I can't give you a sure-fire formula for success, but I can give you a formula for failure: try to please everybody all the time."

~~Herbert Bayard Swope

IX. CHAPTER NINE ~ CREATE MORE ABUNDANCE WITH CONSCIOUS BUSINESS BUILDING STRATEGIES

The secrets to success are not about working harder. Rather, they're often about developing an awareness of how to work smarter. Over the past few years, I've committed to ongoing transformation in my life. As a result I've learned to incorporate spiritual business building principles in all my projects. In the following pages, I'll share some powerful strategies you may not ever have considered.

I used to think that I had to make a choice between having a successful business and living an "enlightened" life—following spiritual and universal wisdom. For a long time, I thought it was "either /or." It didn't dawn on me that I could have both until some years ago, I found that I was working VERY hard for all the success I had, yet there were others around me who seemed to attract what they wanted with ease. The operative word is ATTRACT! I finally realized that these people were tapped into a higher consciousness and used this knowledge to create the life of their dreams. Over the years I've sought to create that same ease of success and in doing so have completely transformed my life. Here are some things that I've learned that have been particularly helpful to me in creating a conscious business:

1. Attract Others To You: Take responsibility for everything that happens to you

Once you REALLY understand that you've consciously or subconsciously created every situation that is happening to you, your perception of the world starts changing. You stop living by default and become much more thoughtful with your actions and your interactions with others. You stop playing the innocent bystander or victim, and start visualizing and expecting more productive relationships and different outcomes in your business dealings. You may not have all the answers, but this higher level of responsibility is more appealing to others rather than the blame game which has a repelling effect. So next time you have the thought that "they did this to me", think again!

2. Allow Abundance to Flow: Create a new relationship with money

The thought of money as a reward is a very strong driving force for many people. It's also a benchmark of success and status. However, the more emphasis you put on it, the more you may actually be repelling it. Money is just energy and has no value except what we give it. When you think of creating wealth, think in turns of what you will do with the money rather than the money itself. Think of clients as people with problems to which you have the solution. The more people you serve, the more prosperous you'll be. This is especially true during the times when you think you really NEED money --- to pay bills, raise capital to launch your company, and so on. With some discipline you can learn to take the "charge" away from it and instead become more enthusiastic about the activities you're doing that will attract money, such as helping others improve their lives. You'll notice everything starts shifting around you and money shows up more freely for you.

3. Attract More Respect: Show up equally with everyone around you

We are all spiritual beings created perfectly equal, yet we may subconsciously feel *less than equal* around those who are paying us to perform a service, people who may have more financial wealth or perceived success, and those who seem to be in a superior position. Do you treat a super-wealthy person differently than someone in your same socioeconomic class? If you met the CEO of a billion dollar company would you be tongue tied? What about meeting your favorite celebrity? You can still respect and admire what they've created but you shouldn't feel less than equal. That behavior will subconsciously cause others to treat you with less respect, which may show up as payments being delayed, missed appointments, lack of recognition, broken promises and so on. If that's happening to you, start showing up more powerfully with this other person and remind them that it's not OK for these things to be happening and you'd like to turn that around starting today. Be equal and supportive, not subservient.

4. Manifest Quickly: Commit to having what you want first

Do you decide to allow yourself to have something once you know how it's going to happen? Especially if it's something you'll have to pay for? Have you been known to say "I can't have that because it's too expensive and I don't have the money for it." True abundance flow when you commit to having something FIRST, even before you know HOW it's going to happen. This works great with money and resources for your business. Without any attachment to how it will occur, continually commit to having whatever you want--- really commit to it without any judgment about the expense, the complexity of it, the logic --- and see how fast the solutions start lining up before you. What seems to be an issue or roadblock today could disappear tomorrow.

5. Choose what would make you happy, not what is always most logical

Your head may tell you that in order to achieve your goals in business you need to do certain things even though it's a struggle, go down certain paths that may overwhelm you, or have relationships with people you don't particular care for...and so you do. I lived like this for years letting my head rule. However, no matter how illogical it may seem at times, when I let my heart make the decisions based on what is giving me the most joy at the time, I create new unexpected solutions. So keep checking in with your heart to make sure you're enjoying your tasks. If you're not, then expect a more abundant solution to appear such as someone offering their services (and allow it), rather than you being miserable doing things you don't enjoy.

6. Help to create for others what you'd like for yourself

This is "give to receive" from a business perspective. Businesses rely on connections, customers, and promotions to succeed. To easily create that for myself, I continuously do that for others by making introductions to resources THEY need, referrals to customers, investing in others, and creating cause marketing opportunities with charities that support the community. It's a continuous flow of energy that constantly loops back to me in a way that's much more magnified from how I originally sent it out. For example, every time I make a referral to someone, it seems dozens come back to me from others. So rather than working harder for myself for accelerated results, I've simply started helping others do the same. It works.

7. Managing too many tasks promotes scarcity

If you regularly think that you're not getting it all done, there's not enough time, and you need to take on everything at once then you're actually sending out a message of JUST THAT. The Universe will agree with you, of course, so you're never really able to catch up until you exhaust yourself.

You're better off learning to manage fewer priority tasks and know that everything will get done in the right time. Non-priority items seem to disappear or become non-urgent all of a sudden or you'll find that other people are showing up more frequently to help you. I remember being guilty of this in the past when I had to-do lists a mile long, multi-tasked even while I was at the gym, and always set myself up to have non-stop workdays. No matter how busy I kept myself, I never seemed to finish my work and regularly beat myself up for it. These days, I work with fewer priority items, yet actually accomplish more during the day. Furthermore, I feel much better about myself and my success has become much more meaningful.

8. There's no real separation between your business and personal life

Don't think you can have your two lives tucked away in nice separate boxes. They really are connected. As you acknowledge and embrace that, your business takes off. So maintaining a balanced, healthy lifestyle with plenty of playtime and an orderly home will spill over into how your business operates. If you allow your relationships at home to remain somewhat dysfunctional or disconnected, you recreate those same relationships at the office or with clients. By the same token, when I feel "stuck" in any aspect of my business, I know to physically unclutter various rooms of my home or office and somehow the business becomes "unstuck".

9. Manifest success by eliminating self-judgment

Ever make a decision that in hindsight could have been handled differently and you carry the thought of "stupid, what were you thinking" around for days, months or even years? Did you ever stop to think exactly how many of those thoughts you continuously carry around with you? It's mind boggling when you really think how hard we are on ourselves. Those thoughts only add fuel to the "I'm not good enough and I don't deserve success" fire. When you replace that with more loving and supportive thoughts, such as "I'm a magnificent human being and I'm doing the best that I can," success flows more easily towards you and it's not fleeting.

⌘　⌘　⌘

"I keep the telephone of my mind open to peace, harmony, health, love and abundance. Then whenever doubt, anxiety, or fear try to call me, they keep getting a busy signal and soon they'll forget my number."

~~Edith Armstrong

X. CHAPTER TEN ~ CREATE YOUR SUCCESS PLAN

A. Miscellaneous support resources

This is a mere sampling of some of the tools and resources to help you create your own brand identity online. You can start with a simple website or blog and progress to a monetized e-commerce site that offers multiple products and services. Links to our most favored (and tested) resources are at www.intentionalincome. com

1. Copywriting resources

Learning how to put together enticing content for your website, E-Book s, Special Reports, and other material., requires knowledge of appropriate copywriting techniques that compel people to take action with your offerings. Qualified people who specialize in copywriting are called copywriters.

2. Shopping Carts

With the right planning and setup a shopping cart helps you sell products automatically. A shopping cart is great for customer follow-up, coupons, sharing your online catalog, and tracking affiliates.

3. Merchant Accounts

Utilize PayPal initially to accept payment and later upgrade to a professional merchant account for reduced fees and to take a variety of credit cards. Affordable wholesale merchant account options are at www.docmurdock.com .

4. Product Development

When you create a video or audio product, you can upload it to your website for people to ultimately purchase and download, or you can create a physical product. I recommend David Schneider at www.SpeakerFulfillmentServices.com

5. Tracking website statistics

Once you start launching product and marketing campaigns, closely track your progress. I recommend signing up for a free Google Analytics account at google.com/analytics and then inserting the provided code on your website pages. You'll see how much traffic you're getting and where it's coming from.

I want to remind you that, as you move forward, make sure it's all about YOU and what you are inspired to create for YOUR life. Make sure the work you do brings you joy and increases your self-esteem, and that it includes the opportunity to help others succeed or live fuller lives. If not, your success will feel empty and will be short lived. Prosperity is directly proportional to all these factors being in alignment in your life.

Don't be afraid to venture out and try something new! This is the perfect time – the resources and technology are readily available, it's easier to access the new skills needed to make a change, investors are looking for new opportunities, people with the talents you need are ready to support you, and new customers are out there for you. Consider immersing yourself in a support program like my *Passion To Prosperity Protégé Program* (www.passion2prosperity.com) which guides you through all these steps in a sequential fashion, including helping you break through any limiting beliefs along the way, so failure is not an option!

B. Review of what's currently in place

Take a few moments to identify all the products, services and strategies currently in place in your business or life to see what can be expanded or what needs to be created:

- How passionate are you and in alignment about what you're doing

- Identify target market

- Current marketing strategies

- Current sales strategies

- Current PR strategies

- Currently a marketing funnel in place with a compelling free offer?

- Technology in place (website, blog)

- Communication tools (postcards? autoresponders? Follow-up calls?)

- Basic product offerings

- Premium product/service offerings

- Continuity programs

- Referral programs

C. Establish next steps

1. Complete a strategic overview of what's in place

Answer all the questions in Step B to use as a benchmark and to see what you have to work with. Follow the path of least resistance and work around what is currently in place, resources you have the quickest access to, or where your comfort level is. However, this is also a good time to start stretching yourself!

2. Determine what your ultimate goals are with your business

You may be ready to take on another role in your business, to plan your exit strategy and do something else with your life, to package it for sale, or invest more time and resources to take it to another level. Be honest with yourself here!

3. Secure your core revenue

Make sure you have at least one primary source of revenue and BUILD upon that by implementing 2-3 marketing strategies previously listed to help increase that revenue. Additionally, focus on creating a basic referral marketing program to increase the referrals coming from existing customers.

4. Create an additional product offering that compliments your core product

If you've provided a service to someone that has completed, can you offer an ongoing coaching program? A wellness or maintenance program? A self-study version of the work you did with that person? A follow-up book or teleclass? What can be easily monetized by you at this stage?

5. Establish your marketing funnel

As you continue to develop infrastructure and create new products and services, don't miss out on the opportunity to build a subscriber list of potential clients. This will be an important function for you going forward. People will buy from who they know so they will readily buy from you if you've taken the time to develop your customer markets ahead of any scheduled product or service launch.

6. Create several free/complimentary offerings

Establish basic product offerings that have value and yet can be offered for free---.an Ezine, Special Report, E-Book , sample products, digital download, or a free consultation.

7. Create Joint Ventures and collaborations

One of the best ways to experience explosive growlh is by cffectively partnering up with people that can promote what you're doing. Take some time to develop those relationships to help you grow your business. Build your team!

8. Make sure your website is optimized

It's important to drive traffic to your website. Have some type of search engine optimization campaign underway to make sure your website is actually working for you. Even if a professional built your website, it may not be optimized with the proper keywords. Order a website checkup at www.docmurdock.com

9. Create opportunities for testing

Create opportunities with whatever you're working on to be able to test your products or services on a small group of people. This provides a controlled way to test everything you're doing and get feedback before you fully launch. *Before* you invest a lot of time and resources in launching or completely launching a program, make sure it's working for you!

10. Create follow-up messages for people in your funnel

When people enter into your system, it should be because they opted in --- giving either online or offline permission. *Never* spam someone you meet who has not given you permission to send them information on a regular basis. For your subscribers, devise a plan of regular communication at not less than monthly intervals.

I've shared a lot of great information with you! It may take a while to fully process it all. My desire is that you stick with this program and gradually incorporate what I've shared. It all works --- just decide what you want to have happen and *commit* to having it!

Plan for your success! Many of these steps require some additional resources and planning to fully implement, but if you set your intention on manifesting, those resources will quickly show up.

I invite you to participate in my step-by-step 16-week **Passion To Prosperity Protégé Program** offered at www.passion2prosperity.com. The support you'll receive will truly help you keep you on track as well as accelerate your progress. Why do I recommend this program for you? Because together we'll develop your Passionate Business Blueprint™, your online and offline marketing campaign, profitable email campaigns for you, and together we'll implement great new revenue streams into your business.

You may also feel yourself experiencing paradigm shifts in the way you thought you should be doing your business, as opposed to all the possibilities that actually exist for you. How exciting! Fears, discomfort, and feeling out of your comfort zone might occur. That's good too, as they can push you forward into a freer zone of creation. We want you to give yourself permission to stretch outside your comfort zone and not judge how you feel about it. The self-judgment and associated fear are what prevent people from changing behaviors that aren't working for them.

Sometimes getting started is not comfortable. Remember, you don't have to be perfect to put yourself out there. Sometimes people think they're not qualified or deserve to receive higher fees for what they offer. Let me tell you, if there's anybody on the planet that knows a little less than what you know, then you ARE the expert to someone, somewhere! You owe it to yourself to share your gifts with others who don't have your knowledge base or have what you have to offer.

It's a great time for you to do some introspection and to get to know yourself and your true passion in life. Once again, give yourself permission to experience all of this. The next few months will be very exciting for you!

Having access to all of this information has made an enormous difference in my life, and I truly wish the same for you! The most important thing is to *get started* ---and remember it never has to be perfect. You'll evolve and grow with each step you take, especially as you allow others to show up and support you.

If you haven't been in "receiving mode" in the past, this is a wonderful time to start. Allow mentors, resources, money, customers...and genuine abundance...to flow easily and freely into your life. Your success will depend on it.

Here's to a passionate, joyful life!

Marie Simone

⌘ ⌘ ⌘

APPENDIX ONE ~ CREATE YOUR OWN MARKETING FUNNEL

<<<Marketing efforts:

_____

_____

_____

<<<Gift & scholarship items:

_____

_____

_____

<<<Basic $-$$ product or service offerings:

_____

_____

<<<Premium $$$ product or service offerings:

_____

_____

<<<Ongoing continuity offerings:

_____

_____

<<< Referral rewards:

APPENDIX TWO ~ GLOSSARY OF TERMS

Affiliate
A person electronically promoting your products and services using a unique link that is tracked back to your website. Payment is made upon completion of a sale.

Autoresponder
A computer program that automatically answers email sent to it and can initiate email on a schedule. You create the preprogrammed messages and business rules for the schedules.

Blog
A "web log" used to comment on a variety of topics and also to post pictures and graphic images. More dynamic in nature than a brochure website.

Cause-marketing
A sales or promotional partnership between a business and a non-profit for mutual benefit.

Continuity program
Also considered a membership program that provides ongoing monthly revenue from dues and fees.

Copywriting
The colorful use of words to PROMOTE an idea, person, business or product. Not the same as reporting or technical writing.

Customer Lifetime Value
The total sales or profit value of a customer over the course of that customer's lifetime.

Demographic Information
Based on the age, gender, life-cycle stage and occupation of consumers.

Ezine
An electronic version of the traditional newsletter format.

Intellectual Property (IP)
Legal term for the creations of the mind such as inventions, graphic images, and written words... IP can be legally protected by obtaining trademarks, copyrights, and patents.

Licensing
To give permission to a person or business to use, package, promote and sell your ideas for a fee.

Payment gateway
An e-commerce application service provider that authorizes payments for businesses by encrypting credit card information and then completing the transaction, connected to Merchant Provider.

PDF
Stands for Portable Document Format created by Adobe Systems. A document becomes "fixed" or "locked" for safe electronic transport that does not allow recipients to modify in any way.

Recurring revenue
Also referred to as passive revenue. Continuous revenue received without a direct effort made by the recipient. Typically received through membership, affiliate, licensing or franchising fees.

Royalties
Usage-based payments made by one party to the other, typically for the use of Intellectual Property (IP) as in the case of a licensing relationship.

Search Engine Optimization (SEO)
The process of systematically improving the volume and quality of traffic to a website from search engines via "natural" ("organic" or "algorithmic") search results.

Shopping Cart Technology
A software program that acts like an online store's catalog and order processor.

Social Networking
A social structure made of nodes (representing individuals or organizations) that are tied by one or more specific types of interdependency, such as values, visions, ideas, financial exchange, friendship, kinship, dislike, conflict or trade.

Target Market
The specific group of individuals sharing some common characteristics (age, zip code, gender, profession) to whom the message is directed. Also called target audience.

Teleclass
A live, interactive workshop conducted over the telephone to a group of participants. Professional conferencing services allow for an unlimited number of participants but long distance changes typically apply.

Webinar
A live online workshop that may present video and audio in addition to live voice.

**GO TO WWW.INTENTIONALINCOME.COM
AND PICK UP YOUR**

FREE GIFTS....

Please register your book at
www.intentionalincome.com to receive a
complete list of my recommended online and
offline technology tools and resources, key
business contacts, how to build a virtual team,
discounted and free services as well as other
FREE BONUS GIFTS valued at over $500!

www.IntentionalIncome.com

People resources
Latest technology tools
How to get the best deals
Free business and marketing resources
"Now money now" strategies
Key contacts
Audio Downloads
How to get corporate sponsors
How to write a book
Free Subscription to "Fast Forward", a business
acceleration ezine

Interested in step-by-step support to create a
multiple income lifestyle for yourself? Start today
at www.Passion2Prosperity.com

www.ingramcontent.com/pod-product-compliance
Lightning Source LLC
Chambersburg PA
CBHW051533170526
45165CB00002B/718